The Top Ten Ways to Drive Your Wife Crazy and How to Avoid Them

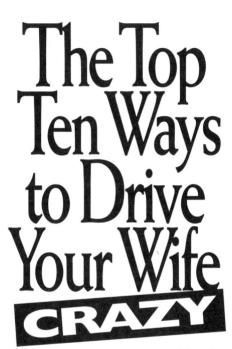

The Top Ten Ways to Drive Your Wife

CRAZY

and How to Avoid Them

Hans & Donna Finzel

VICTOR BOOKS

A DIVISION OF SCRIPTURE PRESS PUBLICATIONS INC.
USA CANADA ENGLAND

Editors: Barbara Williams, Jerry Yamamoto
Design: Scott Rattray
Production: Julianne Marotz
Book Flow/Electronic Production: Elizabeth MacKinney

Library of Congress Cataloging-in-Publication Data

Finzel, Hans
  The top ten ways to drive your wife crazy / Hans & Donna Finzel.
    p.   cm.
  ISBN 1-56476-578-4
  1. Husbands—United States. 2. Wives—United States—Psychology.
3. Marriage—United States. 4. Marriage—Religious aspects—Christianity.
I. Finzel, Donna.
HQ756.F55   1996
306.872—dc20   96-21994
                                                                        CIP

DEDICATION

To our parents
Mark and Anita Bubeck
Alfred and Brigitte Finzel

Thanks for your lifelong examples
of the beauty of what marriages are meant to be

CONTENTS

INTRODUCTION

Once upon a time there was a little blond girl named Donna, who grew up in a family of all girls in the beautiful state of Colorado. She had a warm, loving family, and she decided she would marry her daddy when she grew up—a dream of many a young daughter before reality sets in.

Finally, the day came when Donna realized that she really couldn't marry her dad, so she said to her parents, "Well, then, when I get married, we'll get a trailer and live in our backyard!"

Meanwhile, a little German boy named Hans was growing up in another world. He was the first-generation son of immigrants from the old country, who had landed in Huntsville, Alabama. His dad was busy building rockets to put the United States on the moon.

Hans never met Donna while growing up in Alabama. And he never heard about the business of the trailer in the backyard . . . until later.

As God would have it—in His amazing grand scheme of things—Donna and Hans both ended up as college students in Columbia, South Carolina, in the early 1970s. Hans was actually a senior the year Donna entered as a freshman at Columbia International University. They fell in love, and soon Hans felt it was time to ask Donna's father for her hand in marriage.

On a hot August Saturday in Chicago, Hans finally got up the courage to ask Mark Bubeck for his daughter's hand in marriage. The two decided to meet at the church Mark pastored in Oak Park,

Illinois. Of all places, the fateful moment came while actually sitting and talking on the steps in front of the sanctuary—right by the altar. Hans, experiencing more than just a little sense of unworthiness, felt as if he was asking Moses, the holy man, if he could marry one of his daughters.

"I would like to ask your permission to marry Donna," Hans finally blurted out. With a straight face Pastor Bubeck replied, "I ask just two things of you, Hans. First, I want you to be sure in your heart that this is truly God's will for the two of you. And second, I want you to buy a trailer and live in our backyard." Sensing the panic on Hans' face, he burst into a big smile and filled him in on the family joke about Donna's trailer.

That was twenty years ago. We never did buy the trailer. But we learned quickly that you do get more than a spouse in the marriage deal—you marry into families that have unique cultures and ways of doing things. And you bring your families' values and views into your marriage as you blend both backgrounds into a new hybrid.

We often go back to the fundamental conviction that God brought the two of us together back then in Columbia, South Carolina. And we are committed to our marriage vow that we recited the following summer in that same sanctuary in Oak Park. We are determined to stay together no matter what. We will learn; we will grow; we will forgive; and we will deal with one another out of a foundation of grace.

TOP TEN WAYS?

No matter how much we wish it were otherwise, we all learn best by trial and error. I, Hans, have learned how to operate a somewhat successful relationship with my lovely wife after many years of practicing this principle: *If you don't understand how you do it wrong, you'll never know how to do it right.* We have made a commitment to vulnerability, to feedback, and to making our marriage work amid a world that is rampant with giving up on the old-fashioned institution we call marriage. Our prayer is "Lord, may we never become just another sad statistic."

Let's repeat the principle again:

**If you don't understand how you do it wrong,
you'll never know how to do it right.**

How to see where we get off track as husbands and what to do about it sums up the book you hold in your hands. We're not looking for perfection here, folks. So you can relax. We are looking for positive, growing, nurturing marriages that are actually fun to be a part of.

For some of you, you are already a part of the statistics, and you're trying it again with a better approach. We applaud your courage. Others of you question whether it really was God's will for the two of you to be together. Please read on, and if necessary, seek professional help before you give up.

ANYTHING BUT A PUT-DOWN

So who would want to read this book anyway? Wives buying it for their husbands and leaving it on his nightstand might not be a bad approach. Maybe he just might get the idea that he could learn to be more understanding. And how about you husbands out there who need to rack up more self-guilt? Well, if it's guilt you're after, you've come to the wrong place.

This is not a put-down on men, but a fresh glimpse into our own experience on learning how most women are wired and how their men can run *with* not *against* those currents. We've made these pages an "upper" and positive way for men and women to understand how opposites can live together in a warm, growing, building relationship for a lifetime. Our theory is that all marriages are made up of opposites: one man and one woman, and there you have the difference.

Mistake number one that a new husband makes is that he usually treats her like one of his male buddies. Stay tuned for a big turnoff from her!

I, as the man in our marriage, have always felt that the key to making Donna happy and our marriage last—and prosper—is to really understand this female person I live with. In fact, I have told my three sons on numerous occasions when they cannot figure out some action or feeling of their mom: "Listen, guys, the study of women will be a lifelong pursuit for you. You'll never get to the bottom of her differences, but try as best you can to learn all you can."

One of my pursuits in life as Donna's husband is to figure her out so that I can live in peace with her as my soul mate and companion—not just live in peace, but to prosper and have a lifelong growing relationship. And marriage is supposed to be fun too!

Is It Time to "Do Something"?

Peter Jennings reported on the evening news one night that in the past twenty-four years the divorce rate has multiplied fourfold in the United States. Between 1970 and 1994 the number of divorces shot up from 4 million to 17 million. Too many couples are looking toward breaking up as the solution to a marriage that is not working. That's the modern cure-all—if it doesn't work anymore, throw it away and get a fresh new one that will. We believe that God designed a better way for you and for me.

If you are a husband who feels your marriage is just fine, but your *wife* wants you to "Do Something!" she may be expressing a cry for "help" that is deeper than you would have ever imagined. Have you really heard her and taken the time to study her? Listen to this quote from Gary Smalley: "Who would think of allowing an untrained man to climb into the cockpit of an airplane and tinker with the gauges? Or who would allow a novice to service the engines of a modern jet? Yet we expect men to build strong, loving relationships without any education at all. A man must be 'educated': He first must discover the essentials of genuine love, then practice them until his skills are sharp and natural" (*If Only He Knew*, Gary Smalley, pp. 29–30).

If there is one thing I have figured out so far, it is how different Donna is from me and my maleness. Just when I think I'm getting the hang of it. . . .

On a Dark and Foggy Night

Who would think that something as insignificant as a lost hubcap could create such heat and friction between two civilized, married people? Probably anyone who has been married more than just a few short, blissful months! Anyone can be happily married for a few months or even a couple of years.

It all started on a dark and foggy night on the backroads of Highway 20 in northern Illinois. . . .

Hans' words "insignificant as a lost hubcap" are enough to illustrate the immense chasm in perspectives between men and women on the *same* event!

I, Donna, was returning from speaking in Iowa at a retreat. I was utterly exhausted and spent, yet content and praising the Lord after a wonderful time of ministry and teaching on the New Age Movement. I was returning on Saturday evening in serious fog and rain. Driving on a very winding, dangerous road, I had to concentrate hard just to see the road. It felt as if I was in "the twilight zone". . . this long winding road would never end! As a matter of fact, I was returning home at this time only because Hans had flown out a few hours earlier for ministry in Pennsylvania. Our four children were at home with a baby-sitter until I could get back to them. Hans had given me his cellular phone, which he had only recently received for his work. (Just in case! Of course, men don't *really* believe anything truly serious will ever happen, right?)

After driving nearly three hours under those conditions, I was finally on a smooth and straight portion of road when suddenly it felt as if I was losing my steering. Struggling to keep control, I came to a stop on the shoulder. There I was in the pitch dark along a lonely road in the rain and fog in the middle of *nowhere!* Still in my dress clothes with no flashlight, I got out to check the tires (pounding them on the top). They seemed O.K. to me. I then called "911," but I couldn't even tell them where I was. I prayed and phoned home, where the baby-sitter was barely able to get a few phone numbers for me. Hans had not left a number where he could be reached! I struggled with the normal fears of a woman alone at night on a deserted road, also wondering if a truck would miss seeing me in the fog and barrel into me. As I was praying for protection and wisdom, a woman pulled up alongside to ask if I needed help. She was able to tell me my general location so the police could begin their search to find me. I waited, prayed, and continued calling friends asking for their prayers. It took well over an hour for the police to arrive. With his lights on the van, we discovered that the front right tire on my front-wheel-drive van had "blown" and was badly damaged. He called a tow truck.

As the tow-truck driver hooked up the van, he told me how "lucky" I was to have had such a severe blowout on the *only* smooth stretch of road along that highway. I knew it wasn't luck; it was God's protection! We drove into the small town to his auto shop. The driver was friendly and allowed me to use the phone to try to somehow locate Hans. The van was equipped only with a small temporary tire, and it was impossible to get a new tire on Saturday night. We were still twenty-five miles from "civilization" in Rockford, Illinois, and another long drive from there to home in such weather. After finally reaching Hans, it was agreed that the only reasonable decision would be to have "Dave," the driver, tow me all the way home.

Exhausted as I was, on the journey home in that fog God had

arranged a "divine appointment" with this young man, Dave. He was a young husband and father, and he asked me questions about my teaching on the New Age. He had never heard the Gospel but was very open and interested as I shared the plan of salvation. His wife's aunt, it turned out, is a high-level promoter and teacher for the New Age and lives in Oregon. We finally arrived safely at my home at midnight.

Now for "the clincher" . . . when Hans got home and saw that I was O.K., his first thought turned to the car . . . what is this thing with men and their cars? He looked at the van sitting in the garage and asked, "Did you get the hubcap?" I was absolutely floored! The hubcap? I could have been killed! I had sat in the dark *alone* for one and a half hours and had struggled under exhaustion just to get *home* to the kids, and *all he cares about it the stupid hubcap! Men!*

A few months later, as we laughed about this major flare-up—O.K., I, Hans, was trying to laugh but the wounds were still raw in Donna— my dear, sweet wife asked me, "Hey, Mr. big shot author who everybody thinks is so great, why not write a book on the top ten mistakes that *husbands* make?!" That challenge became the book in your hands, affectionately retitled, *The Top Ten Ways to Drive Your Wife Crazy and How to Avoid Them.*

So I approach our life together with this strategy: to know her is to try to meet her needs. Even after twenty years at it, I often wonder if I have learned anything at all.

Much of our material is drawn from our own twenty-year pilgrimage of seeking to build a strong marriage. Hans has certainly learned how not to meet my needs, and to his credit he has learned some charming ways to fulfill my womanly soul. We also asked married couples along the way—they are everywhere—a couple of simple questions to broaden our perspective. Our desire in these pages is to bring you some keys that will unlock some doors in your relationship leading to a stronger marriage (and a happier wife!).

Hero Husbands We Know

This is not a book about husband bashing. Sure, guys make mistakes, but so do we wives. No one is perfect, and every marriage is a lifelong work in progress.

Throughout these pages we try to be lighthearted about the insensitive things guys do to upset their wives, but at the same time, and in the same breath, we tell about positive examples and good ideas of how to do it right. And each of our ten chapters highlights a "Hero Husband" whom we know or have heard of. From former president of Columbia International University, Robertson McQuilken, to Christian recording artist, Steve Green, and including our own dads, we'll give you inside views of men who do it right. These guys, none of them perfect husbands and fathers, do certain things that make their wives happy to be married. They have listened—learned—and do it right, and we honor them for their gallant attempts to remain forever their wife's knight in shining armor.

Just a Little Love

Of all the things I can do for Donna, I know that first on the list (a literal list I will share with you later), which I keep in my daytimer though I confess I don't refer to it enough, is *affection*. She needs and wants and drinks up my affection and needs it on a regular basis. Like food, she seems to need it every day and can't store it up with an overdose. It reminds us both of the great words of Wynonna and Naomi Judd:

GIVE A LITTLE LOVE

by Paul Kennerley, performed by the Judds
(Used with permission: Warner Brothers Music)

Well, you can buy a diamond ring and slip it on my hand,
Or put me on a big ole plane and fly me to a foreign land,
Show me rows of fancy clothes and say,
"Honey, you can take your pick,"
That would be mighty kind, but it ain't gonna do the trick,

Give a little love, mmmmm a squeeze and a little kiss,
Give a little hug, mmmmm I want some more of this,
Take a little time, yea, and make a little fuss,
That's what a woman wants . . .
So give a little love.

• • • •

One more word of clarification before we begin. Throughout these pages we will tell you stories about people we know and the interesting things that have happened in their marriages. We want very much to protect their privacy. *Every name has been changed for both husband and wife to protect the privacy of those marriages that are trying quietly to make it work.* We thank them for their great input.

You'll also find "Top Ten Tips" sprinkled throughout these pages—small practical ways that can strengthen our marriages. Many of these tips have come from reading good books that have helped our marriage and from friends who have shared their strengths with us.

O N E

MISSING THE LOVE CONNECTION

The Biggest Challenge of All:
Love and Affection

❑ Love covers a multitude of sins. Whatever you
   neglect, don't let it be this one.

❑ In the hierarchy of feminine needs, most men
   know that affection is the odds-on favorite for
   women. It's the doing that is tough.

❑ Women have a deep-seated need for tenderness
   and focused affection—the kind a gentle-spirited,
   kind husband would offer his wife. But what if
   tenderness is tough for you as a man? Exactly
   what is the affection that they seem to crave?

The Beatles were right in the lyrics to one of their first hits, "All You Need Is Love." But why are the simple things in life so complex? When all the votes of the women are in, the results are predictable: "All we need is love." Most men know this about their wives, but the doing of what we know is the tough part.

A Simple Survey of Couples

When the two of us set out to write these pages, we thought ten seemed like a good round number to search for as we sought the top ways that men drive their wives crazy. For men who really wanted to do it right, what were the ten most common errors that husbands fall into in their husbandhood?

We put our lists together based on the twenty years of experience in our own marriage and then began to ask married friends for input from their own experiences. We eventually developed a questionnaire that we sent to quite a few of our acquaintances across the country and around the world.

The results that came back from everywhere were fascinating. No matter where couples live and regardless of economic or social standings, there are amazing threads that run through all marriages.

Among some of the highlights, we learned:

❑ People seem to have the same problems in their marriages, no matter how long they've been married.

❑ People tend to be more forgiving of each other the longer they have been married.

❑ No one has a perfect marriage.

❑ Husbands are quite transparent and knowledgeable about their inadequacies.

❑ Wives, by and large, are forgiving of their husbands, but also understand their faults clearly.

❑ Without a doubt, there is a common thread when it comes to the top issue that creates conflict and difficulty in marriage—which leads us to the point of our first chapter.

Once our research was in, the obvious became very clear: *love is the key*. Perhaps we're restating the obvious, but for us it was good to reaffirm the place of love in every woman's heart. Unfortunately the word "love" is used for everything from "I love these nachos" to "of course I love you, honey." So why is this often used and most popular concept at the root of the needs of every marriage? Let's take a look.

One of the questions we asked the husbands in our survey was this:

The First Question for Husbands:
"What do you think is your wife's number-one
need that you should fulfill?"

Here is a sampling of answers, which became a singular constant chorus:

❏ **From a pastor**: "I find that the quicker my wife and I can get off the surface behaviors to the underlying issues, the better we progress. The greatest single need of my wife is to be loved. I guess Paul had it right in Ephesians 5!"

❏ **From friends on the West Coast**: "Two words sum up her greatest need: 'affection' and 'attention.'"

❏ **From acquaintances in the Southwest**: "This question is a no-brainer for me. She needs my *encouragement by paying complete attention to her.*"

> ## TOP TEN TIP
> *Just Say "I Love You"*
>
> From a wife in Illinois:
> "It may seem like a little thing to him, but I need to be told *every day* that he loves me. I just can't get enough of those three little words—the biggest three words in my heart's language."

❏ **From the Rocky Mountain state of Colorado**: "Sue needs my continual love and acceptance."

❏ **And from California**: "She needs to be cherished, not just through words (although they are critical), but through thought and deed."

This is just a sampling, but enough to see a steady theme of love and affection that comes through loud and clear. Unfortunately, as we anticipated, though we had asked an equal amount of questions—three each—of wives and husbands, we found that the majority of our responses came back from women. Of course men are too busy for such silly things as questionnaires—especially when those questions have to do with such an often guilt-ridden area as your own marriage relationship! We *were* thankful for the men who did write some very helpful responses.

THE POWER OF LOVE

Try this simple experiment. Using the word "love," think of a song that has this four-letter gem in it and sing it. Are you singing? O.K., now try to think of a second song. We can't hear you! Now go for a third. We guess that you had absolutely no problem coming up with your songs.

Isn't love amazing? It is, without a doubt, the theme of more songs that have been written than any other topic, bar none. And some of these songs that come to our minds so easily (too bad we can't remember more important stuff this easily) pack a solid punch. Yes, even country music, which happens to be in the camp of Hans' favorite types of songs.

Even if you are not a lover of country music, please give us a chance with this example. This is a great place to repeat the words of that great chorus from Wynonna and Naomi Judd. Look at these lyrics, study them, and hear what they say. Better yet, get the album and listen to their inspiration!

GIVE A LITTLE LOVE
by Paul Kennerley, performed by the Judds
(Used with permission: Warner Brothers Music)

Well, you can buy a diamond ring and slip it on my hand,
Or put me on a big ole plane and fly me to a foreign land,
Show me rows of fancy clothes and say,
"Honey, you can take your pick,"
That would be mighty kind, but it ain't gonna do the trick,

Give a little love, mmmmm a squeeze and a little kiss,
Give a little hug, mmmmm I want some more of this,
Take a little time, yea, and make a little fuss,
That's what a woman wants . . .
So give a little love.

One of the wives responding to our questionnaire opened her heart wide for us and shared this anonymous insight about her cries for love from her husband, who is actually quite a wonderful fellow. The first question we asked the wives was this:

The First Question for Wives:
"Describe an action, attitude, or habit that your husband practices that frustrates you or hinders your relationship."

She described what she considered a lack of an action, something that is seriously missing in their relationship:

> First there is a lack of touch. I need to constantly remind him to "pretend he likes me" (teasingly) by holding my hand or putting an arm around me or a hug—his family was not very affectionate that way so it is not taken personally. But I still crave that kind of affection.

The more we listen to the basic needs of women, the more we understand the profound wisdom of Paul, a single man who nevertheless was given great understanding about the bond of marriage, who exhorted us husbands in Ephesians 5, "Husbands love your wives."

HUSBANDS LOVE YOUR WIVES

Let's look at this classic New Testament marriage passage in the Book of Ephesians. Paul was lifting love to its highest level when in Ephesians 5, he told us husbands to love our wives as "Christ loved the church."

The more we think about this image, the more challenging it seems to be to apply the biblical mandate. Married love is to reflect in the home the relationship that Christ has to His bride, the church. Listen to the words of Paul:

> Husbands, love your wives, just as Christ loved the church and gave Himself up for her to make her holy, cleansing her by the washing with water through the word, and to present her to Himself as a radiant church, without stain or wrinkle or any other blemish, but holy and blameless. In this same way, husbands ought to love their wives as their own bodies. He who loves his wife loves himself. (Eph. 5:25-28)

The word used here in Ephesians for *love* is the word used in the New Testament for the highest form of love. It is not *eros*, which means mere affection, romantic attraction, or passion, which is what the media usually thinks of when it sings about and displays human love between men and women. No, this is the word *agape*, the selfless sacrificial love that puts others' needs before one's own. This is that kind of love that caused Christ to come to earth in the first place to redeem us as His church.

In Warren Wiersbe's commentary on Ephesians, *Be Rich*, he highlights some of the most important reasons why God designed marriage. Among them:

❑ To meet mankind's *emotional needs*: "It is not good for man to be alone."

❑ To meet mankind's *social needs* to have children and continue the race.

❑ To meet man and woman's *physical need* to fulfill their God-given desires.

❑ To meet the *spiritual purposes* in marriage as the husband and wife experience with each other the submission and the love of Christ.

If the husband takes this model seriously—the Christ and the church example—he will love his wife in these ways. Again quoting Wiersbe:

❏ **He will love her sacrificially**—if he is submitted to Christ and filled with the spirit, his sacrificial love will willingly pay a price that she might be able to serve Christ and glorify Him.

❏ **He will love her with a sanctifying love**—to sanctify means "to set apart," and with this aspect of love their relationship is protected and set apart from others.

❏ **He will love her with a satisfying love**—marriage is meant to be a mutually satisfying experience. Man is not just to get his own needs met, but to nurture a relationship that is truly mutually satisfying. (*Be Rich*, Warren Wiersbe, pp. 50–51.)

> ## HOW MANY TIMES IS TOO MUCH?
> *from Jim Smith*
>
> "I will tell you something else I have learned about women. You cannot tell her too many times a day that you love her. I have never had a woman come to me and say, 'I've got a horrible problem. My husband will not quit telling me he loves me. He just bores me to tears with it. He tells me incessantly.' I do not think a woman can hear that too much. If it is a genuine expression of affection and love."— From *Learning to Live with the One You Love*, Jim Smith, p. 163.

So when we get to the bottom line, love is what women seem to need the most. That seems to be the obvious reason why husbands are exhorted to love their wives in New Testament admonitions. It may seem like restating the obvious, but to listen to wives from Maine to California, it is a modern-day problem for today's husbands as much or more than it has ever been.

Perhaps we husbands need the gentle prodding of the words of Jesus

Himself, "If you know these things, you'll be happy if you do them."

Hero Husbands We Know

Donna and I have known Robertson and Muriel McQuilken for twenty-five years. We first met them before we were married, as young students at Columbia International University in Columbia, South Carolina. Robertson was president of the school, and Muriel was a very gifted woman of God in her own right, who exercised many gifts in many directions both around the school and in other venues.

Muriel McQuilken, in fact, played an important role in bringing the two of us together. Hans was a senior in 1974, and Donna was an incoming freshman. "I'm about to graduate and am unattached, so certainly the woman I will marry is not at this school," Hans reasoned. He and several of his friends were all leaders on the campus that year, unattached seniors about to go out into the world and leave their mark. Then one spring day in early 1974, Muriel pulled aside Hans and his three senior cohorts and said, "Men, there is no girl like a CBC girl [back then the school was called Columbia Bible College]. You better get busy and find one before you leave!"

Well, in fact, Muriel was half kidding and half serious. She did feel that we all four needed a woman of God to stand by our sides as we went out to make our mark on the world. And she must have known that all four of us were already seeing and showing interest in certain women on campus. By graduation, all four of us had found our future mates! And now, over twenty years later, we still thank Muriel for giving us that gentle and wise shove that we needed.

Years later in the spring of 1986, Robertson and Muriel came to visit us in Vienna, Austria, where we were living and working as missionaries to Eastern Europe. We had great days together showing the two of them our adopted city. We noticed right away, however, that something was not right with Muriel. Her memory seemed to have gaps as she would tell us the same stories repeatedly. We thought we knew what might be wrong but said nothing. Soon we would learn that our worst fears were true.

Muriel McQuilken had developed Alzheimer's disease, and today lives with Robertson in their humble home in Columbia. She is unable to speak and care for herself. We have visited Robertson and Muriel several times in their home since this heartless disease incapacitated her and we have been over-whelmed by Robertson's love. To sit and watch him feed her and care for her as if she were a new-born is a humbling experience— love in action from a husband to his wife, who can no longer return the favor.

In 1990, Robertson stunned the evangelical Christian community by stepping down as president of Columbia International University, because his wife needed full-time care. He stated that he wanted to give back to her some of the nurtur-ing care she had provided him for so many years. Over the six years since then, her condition has deteriorated, and Robertson has shown many of us deep insights into the mysteries of love in marriage.

> ## GENUINE LOVE
> *from Gary Smalley*
>
> "If a couple has been married for more than five years, any persistent disharmony in their marriage relationship is usually attributable to the husband's lack of genuine love."
>
> From *If Only He Knew*, p. 74.

It seemed amazing enough to all of us that Robertson McQuilken gave up his career to care for his wife. But even more significant is to see his constant and unfailing love for her each and every day as he cares for her much the way a mother cares for a helpless newborn. The situa-tion has deteriorated from bad to worse in terms of her ability to func-tion at all. Among the many painful effects of this disease is loss of con-trol of most of her bodily functions, and of course she no longer talks.

How can he keep up this kind of commitment? How can you love when there is no payback in return? Listen to these recent words of insights from Robertson, one of our all-time most honored hero husbands. We all wonder how he doesn't get tired taking care of Muriel when he gets no payback from her:

Recently, a student wife asked me that. Cindi has sort of adopted us. As we sat at the kitchen table sipping coffee, she said, "Don't you ever get tired?"

"Tired? Every night. That's why I go to bed."

"No, I mean tired of . . ." and she tilted her head toward Muriel, who sat silently in her wheelchair, her vacant eyes saying, "No one at home just now." I responded to Cindi's question, "Why, no, I don't get tired. I love to care for her. She's my precious."

"Well, I certainly would." Cindi and her husband are handsome, healthy, smart people, and yet she admits that it is hard constantly to affirm one another. What happens when there is so little to commend? How does love make a difference?

Love is said to evaporate if the relationship is not mutual, if it's not physical, if the other person doesn't communicate, or if one party doesn't carry his or her share of the load. When I hear the litany of essentials for a happy marriage, I count off what my beloved can no longer contribute, and I contemplate how truly mysterious love is. (From "Muriel's Blessing" [*Christianity Today*, February 1996], p. 33.)

Powerpoints

The *powerpoints* for this first chapter could be stated in one word: LOVE. But we all know that the *knowing* is one thing but the *doing* is something else. Here are a few tips on getting and keeping the love commitment strong and growing in your marriage:

1. For Both of You:

Learn each other's love languages. Husbands, ask your wife what ways she needs for you to best communicate your love to her. Wives, do the same with his love needs. Make a list—write them down, for these can become your lifelong goals to work on in your relationship.

2. Husbands:

Get out your New Testament and read over the passage on love in Ephesians 5. Then memorize the passage to let the reality of the picture of Christ and His church sink in. Be vulnerable with your wife. Ask her ways that you *do* get your love across. Also ask her what you are *not* doing that you should do to encourage her with language she relates to. Then try to make it a habit to consistently love your wife in the ways she would like to be loved—her love language, not yours.

3. Wives:

In a gentle spirit and without nagging, try to help your husband understand your needs for love. Beyond the needs, help him learn the things he has done well in your marriage to communicate his love for you. Then share with him at the right moments, when he is vulnerable, ways that he can express his love in even better ways.

4. Both of You:

If you have been married for more than five years and you find that there is no love in your marriage, seek professional help. Before you give up, seek help from a solid Christian counselor or pastor that can help you rebuild your love.

T w o

Just Treat Her Like One of "the Guys"

A Lifelong Study of the Feminine Nature

❑ Men: All your life you've had friends who are men, and now you're going to spend your life living with a person of the other gender. Rule number one: *Don't treat her like you treat the guys.*

❑ Women: Does your husband treat you like one of the men in his life? Can't he see that you are different? Help him learn the difference!

❑ The better you understand her femininity, men, the better husband you'll be.

❑ Studying your wife and womanhood must be a lifetime pursuit for the caring husband.

L ike most men, I, Hans, grew up with lots of friends who were guys like me. I did not have many "girl" friends as a young boy—that came later in the teen years. When we're preteen, it is pretty much guys hanging out with guys and girls with girls. The boys do "boy things" like playing with toy guns and tough sports and building model cars. At least it was that way in the '50s and '60s. Today it seems that it is all via video games and electronics, but the nature of the play seems to be the same. Girls, on the other hand, tend to do the "girl things" like riding horses, dressing up, and playing with dolls, jump rope, and crafts. Their play might best be described as the "kinder, gentler" side of the equation.

Now that I have my own young sons and a daughter, I see the pattern of generations repeat itself. Even though what they do has changed, there is still a big difference in what boys do when they are together and what girls do. But one day it all changes—the boys literally wake up to the fact that girls are not so bad to be around—about the same day that certain hormones start kicking in!

Here is where the challenge begins. We begin our social life hanging out with the same sex and learn to treat them a certain way. But when we try to treat the opposite sex the same way, we run into trouble. Young men soon realize that for a young woman there are lots of tender and "female-type things" that he has to learn if he is going to make any progress in the relationship.

Now let's fast-forward to adulthood. Couples get married, and soon the big adjustment begins. Soon after the honeymoon is over, the man realizes that this person he is now living with is quite different than his latest roommates.

During my years in college, I, Hans, had roommates as I lived off campus in various apartments. We guys had certain ways of taking care of our lives and things, and there were rarely conflicts. Each of the guys, no matter how many lived in the place, did his own thing. We're talking total independence here, coming and going as one pleases. Checking in with roommates was really not an issue.

But getting married and living with a female roommate is the dawning of a whole new dimension of experience for most men. Even if you had a sister growing up, that doesn't qualify you for *understanding* life with a woman.

IS THE WOMAN WEAKER?

It was soon after we got married in 1975 that I realized that I did not really know Donna as I thought I did. We fell madly in love that summer of 1974, and after a short courtship, we were married a year later. It is one thing to date and spend a lot of time together, but another to begin the lifelong adventure of marriage—as in living together twenty-four hours a day: jungle breath, messy hair, no make-up and all!

When you date and have a disagreement, you can go home and cool off. Most people in the dating/courtship phase of their relationship go in and out of emotional intimacy. At times you feel real close, and at other times you feel like breaking up. In those down times you can just not see the other person for a while and let things slowly work themselves out. Not so when you are both living in the same house. Among the many new challenges you face, you have to work things out in the here and now—there is no other place to go.

For a man, living with a woman is a lifelong challenge—to do it right and to have a growing and satisfying relationship. *A big way to drive her crazy is to ignore the differences and treat her like one of the guys.*

The Apostle Peter made this quite clear in his first epistle in the New Testament when he said,

> Husbands, in the same way be considerate as you live with your wives, and treat them with respect as the weaker partner and as heirs with you of the gracious gift of life, so that nothing will hinder your prayers.—1 Peter 3:7

TOP TEN TIP

How Not to Blow It

This may seem obvious, but many guys don't see it: "A big way to drive her crazy is to ignore the differences and treat her like one of the guys."

Or, look at these same words in another translation:

> In the same way you married men should live considerately with [your wives], with an intelligent recognition [of the marriage relation], honoring the woman as [physically] the weaker, but [realizing that you] are joint heirs of the grace [God's unmerited favor] of life, in order that your prayers may not be hindered and cut off—otherwise you cannot pray effectively. (From the *Amplified New Testament*, copyright 1954, 1958, Lockman Foundation.)

Before we begin to look at specific things that a man needs to watch to avoid treating his wife like one of the guys, we have to deal with a thorny issue within this passage from Peter. Many women resent or at least don't particularly like Peter's comment about them being the "weaker partner." What did Peter mean here, and is this a put-down of a woman's strengths?

As a matter of fact, I, Hans, can think of many times in our twenty years of marriage when Donna has been much stronger than I. Since confession is good for the soul, here is my list of things where I regularly see more strength in Donna:

❏ In consistent prayer for the family and children

❏ In caring for the needs and concerns of family/friends

❏ In discipline with the children

❏ In tolerance of physical pain and sickness in general

❏ In the courage it takes to deliver four children!

❏ In coping with the physical problems of our children

It is really unfortunate that some ill-informed men have used these 1 Peter 3 verses against women at times to put them down or "in their place." If they would study the words carefully, a wonderful clarification emerges.

Let's take one more look at the passage and take apart a few of the important words:

> Husbands, in the same way be considerate as you live with your
> wives, and treat them with respect as the weaker partner and as heirs
> with you of the gracious gift of life, so that nothing will hinder your
> prayers.—1 Peter 3:7

So what exactly did Peter mean with this "weaker partner" comment? There are several key words in this passage for us husbands to zero in on with a laser focus:

❑ **Be considerate**: A better way to say this would be "dwell with them according to knowledge," or "according to the knowledge you have," as in trying to understand her physical, spiritual, and emotional needs. During the days when the New Testament was written, there were many faulty views of men and women and the marriage relationship—pagan views that were certainly below the view of Scripture. Today we have the same issues in our modern culture, and to fight that we need to dwell with our wives, understanding that we look at our relationship from the view of Scripture and what God has to say about it in His Word.

❑ **Treat them with respect**: Even though, on the one hand, the husband recognizes her weaker power physically as a woman, on the other hand, he should recognize her full equality spiritually as a fellow heir in the grace of God. She deserves his complete honor and is worthy of complete and utter respect as an equal partner in the marital relationship.

❑ **Weaker partner**: The word weaker is *asthenestero* in Greek, referring to physical weakness, not intellectual inferiority. Again in the pagan world, women were viewed as tools to be used. Their status was lower, and they were made to look like slaves to the needs of men. Peter fights that view with his treatment of woman as having her feminine side, which reduces some aspects of her physical strength while maintaining all of her worth and dignity. The husband must recognize that her weakness is physical, not intellectual, moral, or even emotional. In this knowledge it is his duty to care for her and protect her from any physical danger or undue burdens.

❑ **Heirs with you**: This statement should put to rest any accusations that woman is in any way inferior to man in her nature. That is why Peter places the statement here so that we see right away that we are fellow heirs—joint heirs—of all the good things that God holds in store for His children. This statement is best understood with the backdrop of a knowledge of the times when these words were written. Today the court protects a wife's rights, but in ancient days things were not that way. A man would pass on his wealth and inheritance to his sons with no right for the wife whatsoever. But heavenly inheritance is not distributed according to earthly custom—our wives are joint heirs of everything!

How She Differs from the Guys

Clue number one: Open your eyes! But let's get deeper than just outward looks. In our years of marriage I have seen how Donna differs from my male friends in many ways. Some are quite obvious—absolutely great that God made them that way! But some may not be obvious to the average man.

Let's explore some of the differences. This is just a small sampling to get you thinking, and we're sure you can come up with many of your own.

Men and their manners. Now, guys, admit that you have certain behaviors around the men, including the various sounds we emit, gestures we make, and actions we take around our contemporaries, that are really not appropriate at a candlelight dinner with our wives. This would also include how dads act around their sons when there are no females present—a smaller version of the more sophisticated problem when a woman enters the locker room.

Men's crudeness when displayed in our presence makes us women feel belittled. It reduces our sense of your respect for the special relationship we should have apart from you and your male friends. If you have to do these things with your friends, then just bear in mind that we ladies are in another group.

Those "little" comments. These are the sarcastic, cutting remarks meant to be a put-down. For some reason guys find this barbaric way of communication to be macho and endearing to their same sex. For example, a guy will walk into a room, see his buddy with a strange tie, and ask, "Did your mother-in-law give you that for Christmas?" Or "Did you get that tie in high school?"

Now if I made a comment like that to Donna, I don't have to tell you the results. But sometimes we cross this threshold and treat our mate too much like we treat the men. Before opening your mouth, guys, try asking yourself whether what you are about to say will come across lovingly. Let love be the ruler by which you measure your words. Think first—then try speaking to her.

Feedback. One of the toughest questions Donna ever asks me is, "Which of these two should I wear?" That's what I call a lose/lose question. No matter which one I choose, it probably isn't going to be the right answer. What she really wants is affirmation like this: "Darling, they're both beautiful, and I'd really be happy with either one. Which one do you think you want to wear?" When she tells me the answer, then she really wants me to affirm her choice. The same would hold true for earrings and just about anything. So what do I do if she puts on something I genuinely don't like? The answer to that question is simple: Nothing! Enjoy whatever she puts on and affirm her choices whenever you can, because unlike the guys, you have been called to love your wives.

Constructive Criticism. Here's a great story about how not to give your wife feedback regarding her looks or her clothing. Two friends of ours, who must remain *deeply* anonymous even to the general region of the country in which they live, recently told us this hilarious story, which certainly wasn't hilarious at the time. If you figure out who they are, we're dead.

It seems as though the wife had put on some weight due to some physical problems and the medication she was taking. One day her husband, Sam, walked into the bedroom and remarked to his wife, Sara, "Are those panties comfortable?" It seemed obvious from his intonation and comment that he could tell she was having a hard time fitting into things. She said nothing at the time except perhaps a noncommitted grunt. But later she went into what she called a "silent rage."

As soon as Sam left, Sara took out her scissors and cut every single pair of panties up that she had and threw them into the trash—except, of course, the ones she was wearing. She went to Neiman Marcus, the most expensive store she could find at the local mall, marched into the women's wear section, then asked to see the most expensive panties sold. Using the family charge card, she stocked up on the next larger size, top of the line *silk* panties! The next time Sam saw her in these beautiful new panties, he commented on how attractive they looked. "Thanks," she said with a hint of revenge, "they're new. I thought you'd like them. You'll get the bill soon!"

Need we draw any conclusions from this story? What you as a husband might think is an innocent little piece of "constructive criticism" can start World War III in your marriage.

Independence. One principle will hold true chapter after chapter as we look at the things that husbands do to drive their wives crazy. It's the admonition to *love our wives.* Have you ever noticed that Paul rarely exhorted wives to love their husbands? The reason is obvious to a woman: women have a great capacity to love with a loving instinct that causes love to come much more natural to them. For them to express love to a husband is much more natural.

Furthermore, since they are also creatures who need a great amount of love, Paul was inspired to exhort us husbands to love our wives—because we men tend to be independent. We can go it alone on autopilot without a tremendous need for affection. So we are the ones who need the rebuke to love; our wives don't. That is a bottom-line difference between how we behave with the guys—that is, independently—and how we treat that special one who is our life companion.

Communication in general. The best illustration I, Hans, ever heard regarding the difference between what men *think* they communicate to their wives and what their wives actually *receive* came from Gary Smalley the first summer I went to Promise Keepers. Sixty-five thousand men were gathered together in the Hoosier Dome in Indianapolis for a power-packed weekend of male bonding. As Gary Smalley spoke, he asked each one of us to pull one hair out of our heads, hold it up high, drop it, and then let it fall to the ground in front of us. We all did it

> ## HIS NEEDS, HER NEEDS
> *by Dr. Willard F. Harley, Jr.*
> *The Five Needs of Women*
>
> 1. Affection
> 2. Conversation
> 3. Honesty and openness
> 4. Financial support
> 5. Family commitment
>
> *The Five Needs of Men*
>
> 1. Sexual fulfillment
> 2. Recreational companionship
> 3. An attractive spouse
> 4. Domestic support
> 5. Admiration

and were curious about what would happen next. He asked us if we heard the hair as it crunched to the ground. Of course we didn't hear a thing, even though 65,000 hairs fell to the ground at the same time. And you think you have trouble in your bathroom!

Then Dr. Smalley asked everyone of us to take one of our shoes off and hold it high up in front of us. On the count of three he asked us all to drop our shoes at the same time. Well, it sounded like a huge clap of rolling thunder as 65,000 shoes dropped to the floor of the stadium at one time. His point was this: When we think we're sharing a bit of constructive criticism with our wives, we view it as a small little hair we're dropping on her by way of correction. But generally they take it as if we've just hit them over the head with a boot. The moral of the story is this: Men, if you must try to give your wife constructive criticism, remember the hair versus the boot analogy and that timing and tenderness is everything. Wait for those reachable, teachable moments, and don't consider it your calling in life to improve the state of your mate.

THE STUDY OF A WOMAN'S NEEDS —A LIFELONG PURSUIT

In learning to understand the differences of the woman I have chosen to spend my life with, I need to know her true needs. There was a time when I thought that was a no-brainer—any guy can figure that out. But I have learned that Donna is totally different from any male friends I have or ever will have, and I cannot really understand her needs without some help from the outside.

I want to meet her needs so that we can have a growing, nurturing relationship and marriage. Marriage can be the greatest relationship in life—if you learn to meet one another's needs. A real turning point came for me when I began to understand that Donna is wired with an entirely different set of blueprints.

Not too long ago we ran across the best book we have seen on meeting the needs of one another: *His Needs, Her Needs* by Willard F. Harley, Jr. This is one of those *must get* books on surviving and thriving in a marriage. If you don't have it, run, don't walk, to your nearest bookstore and get it!

Dr. Harley is a licensed clinical psychologist and director of a network of mental health clinics and chemical dependency programs in Minnesota. He has had thirty years of experience as a marriage counselor and has counseled hundreds of marriages—many of them in deep trouble. Dr. Harley believes that marriages can be happy for a lifetime. And he has worked hard at helping bad marriages become good marriages, as well as broken marriages become whole again. For those of you who might have experienced the trauma of having one of the two of you involved in an extramarital affair, we especially recommend his book to you.

After reading this amazing book, I decided to personalize it for our marriage. The first insight we gained from Dr. Harley is that marital conflict is created one of two ways:

Couples fail to make each other happy, or
Couples make each other unhappy.

In his book, subtitled by the way, "Building an Affair-proof Marriage," Harley tells of the many couples that fall into trouble with extramarital affairs because of this issue of needs not being met. The good news is that even if that has been your experience, there is help possible. Get his book and learn his valuable lessons. We'll share more of his insights in chapter 7 on building good communication skills.

Our purpose here is not to go into deep marital therapy—we're really not qualified. But we do want to share with you some hints that have helped us in this arena. Specifically, I, Hans, made a list some time ago of the things I can do to meet Donna's needs—to make her happy. Aside from that being the right and honorable thing for me to do for her as her faithful husband, it makes her a whole lot more enjoyable to live with!

Here is my list, based on Dr. Harley's five basic needs of my wife:

How to Meet the Needs of My Donna

Donna's Love Bank

Top Ten Ways to Meet Her Needs:

First of all, the five basic needs she has:

1. Affection: her essential cement of the relationship.

- ❏ Hugs
- ❏ Flowers
- ❏ Greeting cards
- ❏ Holding hands
- ❏ Back rubs (without sex)
- ❏ The goodnight and good-bye kiss
- ❏ Call her during the day.
- ❏ Leave hidden messages while away during travel.

2. Conversation: focused on Donna

- ❏ Never ask, "About what?" if she asks to talk!
- ❏ When I get home, try to get alone with her and find out how *her* day went.
- ❏ Take her out for coffee or lunch.
- ❏ Take a "talk walk" after work.
- ❏ Pursue overlapping areas of mutual interest like camping.
- ❏ Caring partners converse in a caring way.
- ❏ She needs undivided attention breaks.

3. Honesty and openness

- ❏ Truthfulness is the key—period.

4. Financial support

- ❏ Provide for the family's needs.

5. Family commitment

- ❏ I need to be a good and consistent father.
- ❏ Plan to spend quality family time with the whole family, and make sure it is a pattern throughout their growing years.
- ❏ Agree with Donna and engage with her in family standards, rewards, and punishments.

I travel a lot, and when I get home from a trip, there is usually a familiar pattern. I am tired and focused on two things: (1) what happened in the city where I was, and (2) getting back into the mountain of things that piled up for me while I was away.

To fight the battle of neglecting Donna and the kids when I return, I have developed some guidelines to help the reentry process. These are special rules that come into play when I return home. We develop a more complete travel guide for husbands in chapter 5, but here is my short list for starters:

REENTRY

SPECIAL TIPS FOR TRIP RETURNS:

- ❏ Always plan a special debriefing time with Donna over a lunch or coffee away from home. Ask her questions and listen to her answers.

- ❏ Take some time off from work to catch up with my chores around the house.

- ❏ Give her time to warm up to my being involved again in the daily routine.

- ❏ Take the kids off her back for a few hours.

Finally, I have developed a summary short list of things I try to remember to do more than anything else to meet her needs. If I have just a little bit of energy or time for expressing love, I know these are the top proven methods to fill her love bank:

SUMMARY TOP LIST OF MEETING DONNA'S NEEDS: "THE TRIED AND TRUE TOP FOUR"

1. Sit and listen to her day.
2. Bring her flowers.
3. Send or leave her cards.
4. Take the kids off her hands for a spell.

HERO HUSBANDS WE KNOW

Scott is a husband hero of grand proportions. His wife is not well, and he has learned through years of struggle what it means to love your wife and care for her as a "tender" vessel needing nurturing and special care.

Just a couple of weeks ago I, Hans, had the opportunity to attend a special summit meeting on the East Coast of Christian leaders who are in similar types of ministry. Scott was there, but not for long. This once-a-year summit, a small intimate gathering of high-potency influencers, is always something that I look forward to. It's a chance to rub shoulders with men who are in similar positions that I am in, and a great opportunity to receive encouragement. So much of my life involves giving to others, and this is one of the few times of the year that I am on the receiving end and able to receive encouragement from others who understand the unique challenges of my position. I go for male bonding and to get my needs met from other men.

We all arrived at the retreat center in Pennsylvania on a cold evening in February. In fact, Scott and I flew in on the same plane from Chicago. At the airport he called his wife and discovered that she was not doing well with an ongoing illness she struggles with. Later that

night, after we had concluded our evening session, he
called his wife again to learn
that she was not doing well
at all. In the morning after
breakfast we each shared our
personal prayer requests
around the breakfast table.

When Scott concluded his
sharing, he told us that he
needed to take off and go
back home to care for his
wife. It was not that she was
in any critical danger, but
she was feeling very much
alone and sensed a helpless-
ness without her husband by
her side. We laid our hands
on Scott, prayed for him and
his dear wife, and sent him
on his way with our blessing.
He had come all of this way
to one of the most important
weekends in his calendar
year, and then he turned
right around and went home
to stand next to his lifetime
partner and helpmeet. The
nineteen of us who remained
at the meeting agreed unani-
mously that Scott is a hero

"A LITTLE GLANCE GOES A LONG WAY"

Just Let Her Know You Care
from Ruth Ryan

Ruth Ryan, wife of legendary pitcher
Nolan Ryan, recalls the one moment
that stands out for her in Ryan's illustri-
ous 26-year career:

"It probably happened the first time
on the baseball diamond in Alvin,
Texas, in the mid-1960s. Then it happened repeatedly for three decades
after that. Inevitably, sometime during
a game, Nolan would pop up out of
the dugout and scan the stands behind
home plate, looking for me. He would
find my face and grin at me, maybe
snapping his head up in a quick nod as
if to say, 'There you are; I am glad.' I'd
wave and flash him a smile. Then he
would duck under the roof and turn
back to the game.

It was a simple moment, never
noted in record books or career sum-
maries. But of all the moments in all
the games, it was the one most important to me." (From Ruth Ryan's book,
Covering Home, Word Books, as quoted
on page 87 of *Reader's Digest*,
Sept. 1995.)

husband for doing the right thing in a moment like this. She needed his support and his protection in the face of uncertainty, and Scott chose to lay aside his own needs to meet hers. Sounds a lot to us like Christ loving the church in the way He gave Himself for her.

Powerpoints

If you're convinced that your wife is not really just like the other people in your life, then try to sort out some of the ways that she differs. Specifically:

1. For Both of You:

Read 1 Peter 3:7 together and discuss its meaning. What do these words mean to you in your marriage? Look up the passage in several commentaries and write down the explanations that you find. Then read the passage in several other translations.

2. Husbands:

How would you apply 1 Peter 3:7 in your marriage? Take some time to write some notes in your journal about how you should use the truths in this marriage as you relate to your wife.

3. Husbands:

Go through our list of annoying things that husbands do to turn off their wives that we discussed in this chapter under the heading, "How She Differs from the Guys." Do you find any habits here that you are guilty of? Try discussing them with your wife and see how she feels. Better yet, work at being more of a gentleman in private and see what difference it makes.

4. Both of You Together:

Go away for a weekend, or a least overnight, to a nice hotel where you can relax for a quiet evening. Then on the next morning take a couple of hours to discuss the five needs of a wife from Dr. Harley's list. If you are committed to understanding your spouse and meeting her needs, ask her to help you make your personal application list.

5. Wives:

Do not hold any list that your husband makes in good faith over his head as a tool against him. Give him grace and encourage him when he hits a home run. Remember this is a process that can take many months and years to develop.

T H R E E
WINNING ARGUMENTS
IS A LOSING PROPOSITION
Communication and Conflict Strategies

❑ Be careful with your words—they cannot be rethrown like a bad pitch.

❑ The man is used to waging heated arguments in the marketplace—and thinks little of the emotional fallout when it is over. He can have a strong argument with a colleague or friend and forget about it an hour later as they go on their merry way. Not so in a marriage, where the way you say what you say can do more damage than the content of your words.

❑ A woman needs responding more than reasoning when her needs are not being met. Avoid the "I've got to fix her problem" syndrome.

❑ The husband needs to look under the surface when tempers flare and find the source of frustration with tender-loving care.

The night before I was to leave on a long overseas trip to Asia, Donna and I planned a romantic evening. Get the kids to bed early and have lots of time to communicate in all the right ways—if you get the drift.

What ensued was the opposite of what we really wanted most—because of the strange mood I found myself in. I admit it; *it was all my fault.* I, Hans, began a downward spiraling argument about what, we don't even remember anymore, and that was just a few months ago!

In fact, tonight as I write these words, I asked Donna if she could remember what the argument was about. We both remember that it was one of the most hurtful disagreements we've had in years. And yet the amazing thing was, as we sit here tonight and try to remember what it was about, we couldn't. I thought it would be a great illustration to use here, but then I said to Donna, "Wait a minute. Let's not bring it up because it has obviously been buried." Really—the truth—I was worried that we would remember what it was about and start it all over again. But that was not going to be a problem.

Actually, Donna improved on my thought when she said, "No, it hasn't been buried; it's been forgiven and forgotten." That was the beauty of what happened that night: We *did* resolve it before we went to sleep. We would not let the sun go down on our wrath (Eph. 4:26). We would not sleep with it unresolved, nor would I have taken off for O'Hare without our hearts being right with one another. We worked through our misunderstanding . . . even enjoyed physical intimacy before dozing off to sleep. Talk about the full range of emotions.

EXPLORING THE DEPTHS OF DISAGREEMENTS

When I was a young boy, I loved cave exploring. One of the things that I often did with my Boy Scout troop was to go on camp-outs in northern Alabama near forests that were filled with caves to explore. Since these were unprotected caves with no guides, we had to be careful that we left a trail along the way as we explored deep into these dark caverns. In fact, we would usually take some sort of marking system or even string so we could retrace our steps when necessary.

We have found that arguments are very much like cave exploring. Once you have fallen into the depths of a disagreement or conflict with your spouse, there are two options:

(1) *Dig deeper*, accelerate the hurtfulness and dig the wounds deeper, causing
   more distancing (which is equivalent to getting *lost* in the cave, a *real*
   dead end!).

or

(2) *Backtrack*, find your way out and try to find your way back to the opening that led into this cave (back to the origin, shedding "light" on the
   real causes/issues).

Begin the healing process by going back to the beginning of the feelings that led to the hurtfulness. Just recently, while I was balancing the checkbook, I lashed out at Donna for writing so many checks. She keeps a record of the checks that she writes in her check ledger (quite faithfully, I might add), and then I transcribe that information to Quicken software on my computer. I lashed out at her and hurt her deeply that night. The feelings just escalated because she naturally felt defensive about what I was accusing her of.

The fact of the matter is, and I hate to admit it here but I will, in our family she is much more conservative in spending than I am. As we chilled out and calmed down, I realized it was not her spending that caused my frustration, but it was the pressure I felt to balance the family budget when there are so many expenses related to running a large household. I channeled my general personal frustration about the lack of enough money at her. In fact, I've often seen that when I attack her for no apparent reason and we sit back and analyze what is going on, it becomes obvious that she is the one who is closest to me and who happens to be most convenient and "safe" to unload my frustration upon. The frustration is going to fly; she just happens to be the closest target.

> ## FROM ROBERTSON MCQUILKEN,
> *quoting his wife Muriel*
>
> "Once, before we signed off for sleep, I was winning the argument with irresistible logic when she raised up on one elbow, transfixed me with fire in her grey-green eyes, and said, *'Well, let me tell you something. Logic's not everything, and feeling's not nothing.'* "
>
> From "Muriel's Blessing," *Christianity Today* (Feb. 5, 1996) p. 34.

We have met some people who are proud to say they never fight. "Why, Hans and Donna, all this talk about arguing is totally foreign to us. We have such a great maturity and understanding in our marriage that we never argue."

Recently a couple told us that their parents are very proud that they have never fought in their whole married lives. This couple said to us, "You know why they don't fight? Because they have a declared, permanent, ice-cold truce." There is no way a male and a female living together can keep from having some sort of disagreements from time to time. If you're not comfortable calling them arguments, then you probably wouldn't ever use the terminology "fight." Then you might just want to leave it at the concept of "conflict"—O.K., that's a word we can all agree on. Or call them "disagreements."

WHAT'S THE REAL ISSUE HERE?

Let's go back to the major conflict that flared up between the two of us over something as insignificant as a hubcap. Of course, to Hans it seemed insignificant, but to Donna the whole incident was of major proportion in its seriousness. Just to recall the facts, I, Hans, had gone out of town to Pennsylvania to speak at a weekend conference. Donna was on her way back home with the van, after speaking at a women's conference in Iowa. As she drove home, she had a blowout on a dark and secluded road in the middle of nowhere in northern Illinois. Fortunately she did manage to get help, and after quite an ordeal made it home safely around midnight.

> ### TOP TEN TIP
> *Swapping Pet Peeves*
>
> From a creative negotiating wife:
>
> "If you both have annoying habits—and who doesn't—try offering up one of yours for one of his: 'I'll try to leave the mail in one place so you can find it if you'll try not to leave your dirty socks on the floor of the closet.'"

When I returned home and happened to look in the garage, I noticed that the hubcap was missing on the van. I had no clue of the storm that would erupt by uttering these four words: *"Where is the hub-cap?"* Donna was very angry and hurt that I would even think to question her about the location of the hubcap.

I, on the other hand, merely wanted to know if she had looked around for the hubcap while she sat on the side of the road for an hour waiting for a tow truck. "Look around for the hubcap!?" she stated with a rising fury. "You think I'm going to get out of the car in the middle of nowhere in the rain on a dark, empty highway with *no* flashlight in my dress clothes and backtrack along the road to look for a stupid lost hubcap!" The reality and powerful *emotion of her trauma* was having a head-on collision with the *logic of my sense of responsibility* to care for the automobile.

As a further backdrop and for my reasoning, I had just recently replaced another lost hubcap on her van at a cost of $85. I didn't want to think about the cost of another new hubcap on top of the cost of a new tire, and having the automobile towed home. To put it mildly, this was a true blue, state of the art, bonafide, major argument between two people who think they understand each other after twenty years of negotiating a warm and healthy relationship.

Let's take apart the pieces of this argument and try to understand what was going on. Why was Donna so upset at Hans' question about the hubcap? And why was Hans so driven to try to understand why this had happened and what it was going to cost to fix the problem? For Donna, she had been through a dangerous trauma, which she had faced alone in a state of exhaustion in the dark along a lonely highway in the middle of nowhere. What she needed from me was tenderness, care, concern, and empathy for the horrible experience she had gone through. *My question communicated to her that I didn't care about what had happened to her, but I cared only about the automobile.* As far as she was concerned, the *car* was of greater value than the *wife*. Of course, in my way of thinking, nothing could be further from the truth. She was obviously home safe and sound, and everything was O.K.

The immediate problem was that the hubcap was gone. So in my way of thinking, Donna was fixed, but the car was still broken. No matter how logical I might have approached the situation, I put a serious breach in our relationship by lacking sensitivity to her needs. I could have escalated the situation and made it even worse by pressing her as to why she didn't look around for the hubcap. It certainly was going through my mind, but fortunately I had enough sense to keep my mouth shut.

One major thing I *should* have done to show my true love and concern for her (but didn't) was—simply express my joy at her safe return by taking her in my arms and saying, "Wow, I am so glad you weren't injured or worse, honey. I don't know what I would have done if you had been hurt!" By the way, I didn't figure this out on my own. She had to coach me all the way.

AVOID THE "A" AND "N" WORDS

It happened again the other night. You would think after all these years we would learn how inflammatory the "a" and "n" words are. Donna said to me, "You *always* leave the dirty dishes in the sink for me." I can assure you that comment raised my blood temperature immediately. Want to guarantee an all-out war of words with your spouse? Try these two bombshell words as you assassinate the character of the other: "You *always* . . ." and "You *never* . . ."

Now I have to admit that I am

> **TOP TEN TIP**
>
> Want to guarantee an all-out war of words with your spouse? Try these two bombshell words as you assassinate the character of the other:
>
> "You *always* . . ."
>
> or
>
> "You *never* . . ."

just as guilty as she is. On a recent occasion when we were late for an important engagement, and of course I, Hans, was cooling my heals at the back door waiting for her, I concluded it was Donna's fault. I couldn't resist letting the words flow out of my mouth even though I knew it wouldn't be well received, "We *never* make it anywhere on time." Of course, I was implying that it was because of her that we never make it anywhere on time, and thus I was saying directly to her "you are *always* making us late." It was not a pretty sight.

When we try to take apart the dynamics of a situation like that, we realize that neither one of us is telling the truth. There is never a time in a marriage when a situation merits using the words "always" or "never." And yet we like to say those things because of anger that tends to boil up inside of us out of frustration. What we have tried to do as a couple is covenant with each other that we will avoid whenever possible—meaning we'll never try to use it—the "a" and "n" words of "always" and "never." Why are these words so destructive? Because they tend to write off a person in one, quick, heartless judgment. It gives the recipient no hope for improvement and a helpless feeling that it's an area that they are a complete failure in. And since the recipient usually doesn't agree with this statement, it's the perfect setup for a heated conflict.

What would be the right thing to do in a situation like this? The right thing for me would have been to say, "Donna, I am feeling very frustrated about being late to this important engagement. Is there anything we could do to try to avoid this happening again?" And for her, instead of heaping guilt upon me for "never" doing the dishes in the evening, she should say something like, "Hans, I need for you to do the dishes more often. It gives me a real relief for you to do them. I'm also really tired, and it's very discouraging to me to wake up with a sink full of dirty dishes in the morning."

The bottom line is this: Avoid the words that are going to be inflammatory. Instead, try to share with one another how you are feeling, and in a loving and gentle way try to get across to your spouse what specific change they could make to improve the situation. It's not the natural approach that any of us take because of our own selfish natures, but it is the high road of maturity, which will make for a much stronger relationship.

WHY TEMPERS FLARE

In our experience and study, we've learned that any couple who never argues or has a disagreement in their relationship is usually in deep denial. Hopefully, as a couple matures and adjusts to one another, the frequency of conflicts will lessen through the years of marriage. But the reality is that when two people live so closely together and deal with the pressures of life, they will have conflicting viewpoints and attitudes from time to time.

We have isolated the most *common* reasons for the escalation of conflict between husband and wife, which are these:

❑ **Needs not being met**—If conflict arises over something that seems insignificant or trite, before allowing tensions to escalate, *look deeper!* Ask, "Is there something I have done to offend (or hurt) you?" If not, ask, "Are you feeling pressure from something that I could help relieve?" Usually you will discover a deeper issue that needs attention (remember coming out of the cave into the light of "origin").

❑ **Differing expectations**—Communication is the key to preventing conflict. Stop before reacting, communicate "where you are coming from," and ask your spouse to share their perspective or outlook. Taking the time to share your expectations regarding a given decision or problem and making the effort to understand one another will often resolve the issue. The radical differences in perspective may not easily be understood, but we *must* come to accept one another as part of mutual submission in love. (Eph. 5:21—"Submit to one another out of reverence for Christ.")

❑ **Displaced anger**—Stress from outside sources: overwork, demands and needs of children, financial concerns, fatigue, all may come out toward our spouse—the "safe" one to "vent" on. Stop! Remember, angry words will only escalate the situation. Tell your partner what it is you are really dealing with, and allow him or her to "bear your burden" with you! Who better to do this than our mates? "Carry each other's burdens, and in this way you will fulfill the law of Christ" (Gal. 6:2). The "law of Christ" is, of course, to *love* one another! (James 2:8)

❑ **Violation of rights**—Mutual respect for one another is the bottom line here. *Assume* little! Each of you must have the perspective of your spouse. Make a practice of talking through *all* decisions that affect the family together. This should be an inviolable rule. It relieves pressure on either partner when they are under pressure to decide something alone.

❑ **Personality conflicts**—Find ways to meet each other halfway when your basic tendencies cause conflict. Both must give and not expect their mate to be the only one to change. For example, I, Donna, have adjusted as a *very* open "people person" to Hans' more private ways by not "bearing all" to "everyone." I am more selective with whom I share our family and personal information. Hans, on the other hand, has adjusted his naturally hard-nosed "Germanness" to work on being more tender, expressive, and showing loving concern if I'm not feeling well.

❑ **Dramatically different family backgrounds**—Hans' studies in "Corporate Culture" were very helpful to us in this area. Although we had already adjusted to one another's differences in many ways, we didn't truly understand the *impact* of "Family Culture" until we had been married fourteen years! We have a true "cross-cultural" marriage with Hans having been raised in a strong German subculture in Alabama while I was raised in a very American and emotionally open Christian home. My family expressed love constantly and openly. Meanwhile, the German people as a culture do not openly express their love.

We strongly believe that this area of "Family Culture" gives us our most basic instincts. As no two families are alike, *every* marriage *will* have "culture" conflicts that must be worked through. "My way is the right way" is a natural way to feel, but it takes maturity on the part of both in a marriage to adapt and give up some of those ways that offend or conflict with our spouse. Our godly professor Mr. Buck Hatch at Columbia International University used to call some of those ways, "Tremendous Trifles"—such as the particular way we squeeze the toothpaste. He confirmed that they are only the tip of the iceberg of what lies below—the basic culture and way of looking at life that each one of us have. Each one is unique. We believe that by "becoming one flesh" and "leaving and cleaving," the Lord can help us study, accept, adapt, learn from, and even *love* those differences in each other. But it takes commitment and work, and it must be looked at as a mutual journey of discovery.

HERO HUSBANDS WE KNOW

This story is not really about healing conflicts, but more about being insensitive, which is a root cause of disagreements and unhappiness in marriage. Ron and Jamie have been married for seven years. For six of those seven, Ron has done zip for Valentine's Day. Maybe he figured that he got his valentine and married her. Thus, there was no need anymore to make a big deal with red hearts and roses. Wrong!

How does Jamie feel when Ron does nothing? Unappreciated at least and unloved as well. Many women feel a sense of being taken for granted by their husbands when they act this way—or fail to act. She starts to feel like the TV or the furniture or refrigerator—just another one of the conveniences in his life that he has ready and waiting when he needs it.

Finally, after all these years of neglect, Jamie got through to Ron that it really made her feel unloved and unnoticed that he did nothing on Valentine's Day. I'm not sure if it was a sledgehammer or a crowbar, but the message finally got through.

I think what Ron did deserves our hero husband reward for Valentine's Day. First, he took the day off from work. Second, he asked her to go shopping at the places of her choice—ended up going through lots of those little feminine stores with lots of knickknacks and fancy frills. Ron would have preferred the hardware department at Sears, but he hung tough and spent several hours with her going through the shops.

But that's not all! Ron called one of Jamie's best friends a few days early to do some research. This guy really went all out! He discovered that Jamie was tired of her hair the way it was and wished so much for the chance to try something totally new—a complete makeover. But since she knew it was out of the question with their budget, she didn't even bother. Well, after the shopping time in the early afternoon, Ron surprised Jamie and took her to a fancy hair styling salon downtown for a complete hair styling makeover. What a hit! Home run with Jamie? Absolutely. He filled her love bank and communicated in loud tones that he loves her and the role she plays in their marriage.

One postscript on this story. One of the smartest things Ron did was call a good friend of Jamie's and ask for advice about how to communicate that he really loves her. We have seen men do things that they think will make their wives happy only to bomb out and make matters worse. Don't be too proud, men—ask an expert: a woman.

Powerpoints

The best way to work out an argument is to take the following steps:

1. Stop the hurtful words.
2. Cool off.
3. Reflect on your feelings.
4. Ask what's down deeper.
5. Don't let the sun go down on your wrath.
6. Forgive and forget.
7. Seek help if necessary.

If you have a pattern of consistent arguments and conflicts in your marriage, you should probably seek professional help from a pastor or counselor. We would also encourage you as a first step to look at our list of "Why tempers flare" earlier in this chapter and try to identify what causes conflict in your marriage. Perhaps you can find the right teachable moments to discuss the list together.

> **WISDOM FROM SOLOMON**
>
> "Starting a quarrel is like breaching a dam;
> so drop the matter before a dispute breaks out."
> —Proverbs 17:14

A few final thoughts on finding a "Win/Win" situation in marriage. Make *praise* a practice in your marriage! It is so much easier to see the problems and weaknesses in our mates, and it's common to let stress overcome us and just simply react to our circumstances. That's where conflict gets to be a habit—an easy, lazy reaction. Ask the Lord to remind you to Praise, Praise, Praise your wife. Gary Smalley reminds us of the great power of praise: "I can vividly remember my boss saying years ago, 'If only I had ten men like you, we could change the world.' After that, I was so motivated I couldn't do enough for him."

Teachers know how praise motivates children. One teacher said she praised each student in her third-grade class every day, without exception. Her students were the most motivated, encouraged, and enthusiastic in the school. When my high school geometry teacher praised me regularly, my "D" average climbed to an "A" in six weeks.

Knowing how significant praise can be, why do we as husbands fail to express it to our wives? Several reasons. The most common is preoccupation with our own needs, vocation, and activities. We lose sight of the positive and helpful qualities in our wives when we are preoccupied. Even worse, we fail to acknowledge our wives' helpful traits when we do notice them.

When a husband forgets his wife's need for praise, the marriage is usually on its way downhill. So how can we grow in this area of encouragement and praise toward our wives? Make praise a practice!

❑ **First, praise the Lord!** Praise Him for *your* wife, the one He's given *you.* Remember, the only thing that was "not good" about God's creation was that Adam was alone! Psalm 92:1-2—"It is good to praise the Lord and make music to Your name, O Most High, to proclaim Your love in the morning and Your faithfulness at night."

❑ **Second, praise your wife!** When you think about your wife, dwell on those things in her that are true, noble, right, pure, lovely, admirable, excellent, and praiseworthy (Phil. 4:8). Certainly the "excellent wife" in Proverbs 31 was very "together" and successful largely because her husband believed in her, and his love overflowed in praise! "Her children arise and call her blessed; her husband also, *and he praises her:* Many women do noble things, but you surpass them all" (Prov. 31:28-29, italics added). *Wow!* Any woman would respond positively to that kind of statement!

Ask the Lord to remind you to do this. Although it may not come easily, He has commanded it. Therefore, He *will* help you as you draw on *His* strength.

F O U R

LET MOM HANDLE THE SPIRITUAL STUFF

The Man's Role of Spiritual Leadership in the Home

❑ Men are intended to lead the spiritual way in the
   home, but it seems to fall more naturally on the
   wives and mothers who do so much to raise
   the children.

❑ There are logical reasons why it is hard for men
   to assert spiritual leadership on the home front.

❑ The worst thing a wife can do is to chide or prod
   her husband to be more of a spiritual leader in
   the home. She needs to help him in other
   supportive ways.

Not long ago we attended the funeral of a spiritual giant, who had passed away after a long and fruitful life of ministry. As one tribute after another was given to this man of God, the topic of his early spiritual formation was repeated over and over. You guessed it, it was his mother who had the most powerful influence on his life in his tender, growing-up years. When you hear story after story like this, you can't help but ask yourself, "Where was Dad?" Is he some kind of an absent jerk who just doesn't care about spiritual things related to his children? Or are the issues deeper? Why is it that so often Mom is left to handle the spiritual stuff for the family?

How many times have I let Donna take the spiritual lead in our home, because I come home tired or I have been away on a business trip. Since she just seems to be more aggressive in wanting the kids influenced with spiritual input, I just let her keep taking the lead. I know it is not ideal, but sometimes I just don't have the energy to do what I should.

THANK GOD FOR MOMS AND GRANDMOTHERS

Several years ago we watched an in-depth interview by David Frost of Billy Graham on public television. It was an unusual interview because Billy Graham allowed David Frost to ask anything he wanted, no holds barred, for an intensive and thorough two-hour interview. Among the comments that had the most profound effect on us as we listened were his comments about the spiritual impact he had on his children. David Frost asked Billy Graham what he regretted the most as he looked back over his life. Without hesitation, Dr. Graham commented that his deepest regret was that he had not spent more time with his children. He spoke of the godliness of Ruth Graham, who had raised the children while Billy was out reaching the world through his evangelistic crusades. No one would fault Billy Graham for the marvelous work he has done, but it was a moving reminder to hear him look back on his life and regret that he had not been more active in the spiritual upbringing of his children.

How many people do you know who attribute their spiritual upbringing to a godly mother or grandmother? We have known many. It is the pattern, but it is not ideal. Actually this common approach of husbands undermines the spiritual moorings of children, who need strong signals of spiritual leadership from their dads. The father's spiritual input is crucial for the development of children. But it is the mothers who tend to be more involved in raising the children and can end up filling the vacuum of spiritual leadership. This seems to hold true of working mothers as well as the stay-at-home moms.

When it comes to spiritual tributes given by children to their parents, it seems that nine times out of ten it is Mom who gets the adulation. If a person has grown up in a Christian home and you ask that person who had the greatest spiritual influence on him or her, isn't it amazing how often that person refers back to his or her mother? For a number of important reasons, which we will explore in this chapter, moms seem to be the ones who end up having the most spiritual input in the lives of the children during their formative years.

THE BEST OF INTENTIONS

I, Hans, consider myself an average spiritual father. In fact, I've been to Bible college and seminary, and perhaps might be considered by many to have "above average" spiritual potency. And, of course, I am totally committed to the nurture and admonition of my children in the things of the Spirit. However, our family falls into the same trap that many other Christian homes fall into, where it seems as if Mom has the most spiritual impact on the children. How do I know? Just ask our four children—Mark, Jeremy, Andrew, and Cambria.

If you were to ask our children why they believe what they do, how they have formulated their spiritual outlook on life in terms of who has influenced them the most, and where they get their spiritual data, I have no question in my mind that they would say they got it from their mom. I want to be the spiritual leader in the home, but there are a number of practical reasons that seem to fight against it.

> ### TOP TEN TIP
> *Seize the moment!*
>
> Make the time, and tune into those teachable moments with your kids. Share your heart! Be sure you *tell* your kids your testimony, and explain *why* you choose to do what you do (go to church, *not* go certain places, etc.). Be sure to pray together with your kids about their problems, or particularly tough situations. And ask them to pray for you for specific needs or requests you have as well.

You know things get bad when your eight-year-old second-grader goes digging through the cabinet, pulls out the family devotional Bible, and brings it to you saying, "Dad, could we please read another story tonight?" Talk about being put in my place! Or take my second-grade daughter, who usually begs me in the evenings when I tuck her into bed to pray with her. Confession is good for the soul, and thus I offer you this transparency.

The fact is that by the time I have put in my day of work, come home, and dealt with all of the things related to taking care of the house, taking care of bills, dinnertime talk and eating, fixing whatever is broken, going through the mail, and helping with homework, I am exhausted by the time the kids are ready for bed. There are those things that I know I should do, but they often wage war against that which I have the energy to do. What I should do is read books to them, tell them stories, pray with them, and have in-depth conversations discovering how their day went.

With our four children you can imagine that it can take quite awhile going from room to room and child to child through that long process. I call our upstairs hallway where they all sleep, our dormitory, and walking up and down that hall fulfilling their needs is one of life's biggest challenges. It would really be nice to also have a few moments with Donna to try to keep that relationship nurtured and alive. Yet a man often feels that he has little or no time to himself.

Mature Christian fathers know that they should be the spiritual leaders in their home. I know that, and my counterparts know that. But in reality, so many things fight against the best of intentions. Some of the big reasons are:

❑ **Fatigue**—Never underestimate the fatigue factor. We leave for work early in the morning, put in a hard day slugging it out at the office, pouring our energy into our life's work, and usually come home tired, fatigued, and at least ready for some relaxation. The best word that I can find to describe my feelings when I get home in the evening is "disengagement." I am engaged all day aggressively, pursuing my work and just wanting to have some downtime to do nothing. I never live the

"My Three Sons" type of evening with slippers, the easy chair, and the evening paper. But I would be dishonest if I said I wouldn't love it once in a while.

- **Distraction**—Another thing that is difficult for a working man to do is to change gears from what he has been consumed with all day at his workplace to the issues that are raging about on the home front. It is hard to turn off the things that you thought about all day, and to turn on family life when you walk through the door at home. Years ago I had a professor in seminary who mentioned that every day when he went home from teaching, he had tried to leave his troubles at the roadside by a certain bridge, which he passed on his way home. He would throw his troubles over the bridge and pick them up on his way back to work the next morning. It is a good illustration of what we should try to do to shift gears from the distraction of work to the needs of our spouse and children at home. But the fact of the matter is, it is difficult to make that shift.

- **Despair**—As Erma Bombeck said, "Guilt is the gift that keeps on giving." Many of us Dads feel downright guilty and despondent by our lack of spiritual leadership in the home. You don't have to tell us that we're not doing what we should do . . . we know it all too well. And the worst thing a wife can do is to chide or prod her husband to be more of a spiritual leader in the home. She needs to help him in other ways we will get to in a moment. When I talk to fellow fathers, there seems to be the common feeling among most of them that they are failures at doing all that they should do to be the spiritual leaders in their homes. A despair can set in that makes you give up even trying.

- **Inadequacy**—Along with feelings of despair is the complementary sense of inadequacy. Most of us don't feel that we are all that spiritually tuned up to be the great devotion leader, prayer warrior, and spiritual giant in the home. We have our own struggles, and after the hard day at work, we simply find little or no reserve from which to draw spiritual strength for our family. At times I ask my children to take the lead in family devotions and they love it!

❏ **Absence**—For many dads, they are just downright absent when Mom is not. Just as with the illustration of Billy Graham, as much as he wanted to be a strong influence in his home and to be a spiritual leader, he was just away from home too much to be that for his children. In my line of work I travel often and will be away for days at a time. So Donna is left at home to be the one who is always there on a regular basis, day in and day out, to care for the needs of the children. She is the one who is there to consistently understand their needs, to pray for them, and to talk with them when spiritual issues come up. When I do return home from a trip, it takes me several days to get reacclimated to family life. It is impossible for me to immediately pick up the mantle of leadership the moment I walk in the door. In fact, that itself is a cause of friction between us, as Donna is ready for me to get home so that she can be relieved of the total weight of family responsibility.

FATHERS AS SPIRITUAL LEADERS

So where do we get the idea anyway that it is up to the dads to be the spiritual leaders in the home? We begin in Scripture with the whole foundation of the Old Testament and the Jewish home, where the father was actually the teacher of the children. Public school and classroom outside of the home is actually a modern invention. Historically the parents, and particularly the fathers, were very much involved in training the children to prepare them for life.

Of course, the classic New Testament verse is found in Ephesians 6:4, where we read, *"Fathers, do not exasperate your children; instead, bring them up in the training and instruction of the Lord."* When Paul wrote these words to fathers, he no doubt had the Old Testament in view as a backdrop to this admonition. Paul states very clearly that it is the father's respon-

sibility to bring up his children in the "training and instruction of the Lord." *The Bible Knowledge Commentary* magnifies the meaning of verse 4: "Fathers are addressed because they represent the governmental head of the family on whom rests the responsibility of child discipline." The commentary goes on to explain that the meaning of "do not exasperate" is "do not provoke to anger." This can be done to our children by "unreasonable demands, petty rules, or favoritism. Such actions cause children to become discouraged." Then the passage goes on: "Instead, fathers are to bring them up, that is, rear or nourish them ('provide for physical and spiritual needs') in the training ('child discipline,' including directing and cor-

> ### THE PROTECTORS
> ### OF HOME
>
> "God put a father in the home to be the protector of that home, to shield his wife and children from destructive influences. What we as fathers allow to come into our homes will either have a positive or negative effect on our families. God wants a father to be very sensitive to this so that the atmosphere of his home is conducive to raising children who love Christ and desire to follow Him."
>
> From Jim Logan, *Reclaiming Surrendered Ground* (Chicago: Moody Press, 1995).

recting; 'training in righteousness' and God's 'discipline' of believers) and instruction of the Lord" (*The Bible Knowledge Commentary,* Walvoord/Zuck, p. 642).

Men, we need to take very seriously our role as protector of our home in the spiritual realm as well! Are you using biblical discernment in what movies, magazines, and other influences you are exposing yourself to?

Are you doing the same with your family in the choices you allow them to make in music, video games, the Internet, and other activities? Jim Logan, an excellent family counselor, gives powerful warning to dads about this issue in his book, *Reclaiming Surrendered Ground*.

First, Logan points the finger squarely at Dad: "God put a father in the home to be the protector of that home, to shield his wife and children from destructive influences. What we as fathers allow to come into our homes will either have a positive or negative effect on our families. God wants a father to be very sensitive to this so that the atmosphere of his home is conducive to raising children who love Christ and desire to follow Him." Jesus spoke of this principle when He said, "In fact, no one can enter a strong man's house and carry off his possessions unless he first ties up the strong man. Then he can rob his house" (Mark 3:27).

In Jim Logan's work with many troubled teens, he has found that "In order to spoil a home, Satan has to attack and bind the father, the 'strong man,' and then go after his family." So when he is counseling a troubled child or teen, he first must find out what shape the father's spiritual life is in! Therefore, be *sure* your own life and mind are pure and right with God. Live and lead your home by the power and love of the Holy Spirit (Gal. 5:19-26). Jim also points out that a child may still choose to willfully rebel against a godly father and mother because of his or her own free will, but the principle is nevertheless crucial and valuable to practice (*Reclaiming Surrendered Ground*, Jim Logan, pp. 121–22).

Let's take a moment to look at some Old Testament admonitions for the father to be involved in the spiritual upbringing of his children:

❑ **Father Abraham**: God Himself said to Abraham, "For I have chosen him, so that he will direct his children and his household after him to keep the way of the Lord by doing what is right and just, so that the Lord will bring about for Abraham what He has promised him" (Gen. 18:19). We see a direct cause-effect relationship between Abraham's responsibility in directing his children and his household to keep the way of the Lord and the resultant blessing and promise, which the Lord had given to Abraham and his descendants. This promised blessing is a *gift* we give our children (and grandchildren) as we live godly lives and train our children in godliness! Psalm 103:17—"But from everlasting to everlasting the Lord's love is with those who fear Him, and His righteousness with their children's children."

❑ **Ten Commandments**: In accordance with the Ten Commandments, the guarantee that generations to follow would love the Lord their God was dependent upon the fathers' passing down to their children an understanding and a love for the law of God. Deuteronomy 6:6-7: "These commandments that I give you today are to be upon your hearts. Impress them on your children. Talk about them when you sit at home and when you walk along the road, when you lie down and when you get up." It is clear from the context that this admonition goes directly to the elders and fathers of Israel.

❑ **Solomon's wisdom**: Finally, in the classic text from the Book of Proverbs, which were the words of wisdom of Solomon to the fathers of Israel, we find: "Train a child in the way he should go, and when he is old he will not turn from it" (Prov. 22:6). What could be more obvious than this admonition for a father to be actively involved in the process of training the child in the ways of God?

It's just not fair to your wife and to your children's mother to have her carry the spiritual ball in your home. It is also not fair to the kids to expect Mom to be the spiritual anchor in your home.

The dangers of relying on Mom to handle the spiritual stuff include:

❑ Kids won't have a strong example of God as their Heavenly Father.

❑ Dad getting away with avoiding his God-given responsibility.

❑ Putting too much pressure on Mom that God never intended.

❑ Providing a bad example for sons and daughters who will grow up one day to be parents themselves.

HERO HUSBANDS WE KNOW

I, Donna, look back on my childhood with great joy and some awe at my parents. My father was a busy pastor. In the first thirteen years of my life, our church grew from a group of 50 to over 600 members. My mom, also involved in music and ministry as a pastor's wife, was a full-time homemaker. She carried much of the weight of raising three daughters. She knew how to let go, though. She instinctively knew the importance of allowing her girls to be very close to their daddy. We all were. Although each of us felt unconditionally loved and treasured by our dad, we all knew that he loved us equally.

The close relationship we had with him started when we were very young. I remember the story my parents would tell of the time when my older sister, Rhonda, was a "tow-headed" toddler. Dad was closed away in a room at the front of our house and deep in study for his sermon. Rhonda was busy playing, but she kept trying to interrupt Daddy to try to get him to play with her. With some frustration, he tried to tell her he must be left alone to work. With her simple "babytalk" words, Rhonda said, "I just want to be with you, Daddy." Wisely, Dad set aside his work for a short time to take Rhonda in his arms and "be with her" for just a few minutes. That was all she needed, and she was off, blonde curls bouncing behind her.

Unlike so many other pastors' kids, or "PK's" for short, we all grew up loving the ministry. We all loved our church and felt a part of what our parents were doing. We truly were at the church, which was adjacent to our home, every time the doors were opened. Our church *was* home. We *loved* it, and all of the people were our extended family.

We had our daily devotions after supper as a family. Usually Dad would read a Bible story and ask us questions to see how well we had listened. Then we would pray together. Our home was always open to others. We had missionaries, families, and those in need in our home on a weekly basis. Dad and Mom lived the same whether visitors were there or not. The Lord was the center of our lives, and serving Him was the outpouring of our love for Him. No artificial "because *you* are the pastor's kids" laws were laid on us. Any rules or behavior expectations were always well explained (and demonstrated to us). The bottom line was always that we are believers, and our lives belong to the Lord. *He* is the reason for all of our choices and actions.

Life in our home was always busy. Dad traveled a few weeks a year to speak at meetings in other churches. The phone would daily ring off the hook with calls from

> ## ON OUR IMAGE OF GOD COMING FROM OUR EARTHLY FATHERS
>
> "Recently, I heard a wonderful message where the speaker asked us all to do something unusual. He asked us to picture in our minds the Lord's arms. He illustrated many ways we might picture them. Many would picture them closed in front in a position of retribution or disapproval. Some would picture them open in a welcoming way. My immediate picture to my surprise was of my *own father's arms* enfolded around me in a loving, safe, accepting, secure embrace."
>
> —Donna's reflection on her father

church members and people around the world with questions or problems. My dad was the consummate pastor with great gifts in counseling and prayer. Dad always called on *each* person from our church who was in the hospital, no matter how many hospitals he would have to drive to. Then there were always evening board meetings, but Mom rarely complained. She made it a point to find great joy in the ministry herself, and she refused to allow a negative attitude toward Dad's busyness spill over in anger at her lot as a pastor's wife.

Much of my dad's spiritual leadership to us occurred in the natural daily happenings of our lives. He was very strong in disciplining us! It was, however, *always* tempered by his unshakable love and acceptance of us. We knew the boundaries, and Dad was always extra creative in discipline if we overstepped a boundary in relationship to honoring the Lord. The most painful and powerful one I remember was when I was about ten or eleven. My sister, Rhonda, and cousin, Jan, were both older than I. Since our home, the church parsonage, was right next door to our church, we would often go over to the church gym to play or ride bikes around all of the sidewalks. One sunny afternoon, we were in the church sanctuary "hopping" pews! It was great fun, racing from pew to pew using the pews as hurdles. But then Dad walked in. *Boy* were we in trouble! Our punishment for such wanton disregard for the holiness of our place of worship was to have us pull all of the weeds bordering our whole church parking lot the rest of that summer day. Each of us was given a section to pull. Since we had to show our own pile to him, we spent the day basically alone with our thoughts and work far away from one another, each working hard. Never again did any of us consider misusing our place of worship.

As we grew into our teen years, our relationship with our dad became even more important. I respect my mom so much for having the wisdom and maturity to let us be closer to our dad than we were to her at times. Those early foundational years of his spiritual leadership and open relationship were key! We had *always* known that no matter how busy Dad was, *we* came first. Our weekly family nights and yearly vacations had further given us time to build a strong foundational relationship with our parents.

The security we felt in our father's love and openness of sharing carried over into the rocky teen years. When I struggled with a relationship with a boyfriend or the temptations thrown at any teenager, I could talk to Dad. Unlike most of my friends, I didn't have the desire or need to turn to cigarettes, beer, marijuana, or sex to find happiness. When I was down, I knew I could turn to my parents and to the Lord, who gave me all I needed. My friends were dumbfounded! Why not just *one* puff? Why not just *one* drink? It was obvious they did it to feel a high, to feel better . . . but I felt just *great* without it. Yet even in those times when I would be in a period of rebellion and not close to the Lord or to my parents, Dad did it right. Sometimes he'd just say a simple, "Gettin' kinda cocky, young lady." Coming from him, those words would cut through quickly. But more often, Dad would just entrust me to the Lord in prayer. Neither he nor Mom would say anything to me directly. They would simply pray about my rebellious spirit. Inevitably, the Lord would use other means or just convict me by His Spirit, and I'd repent. Then when I'd go to tell my parents of my renewed joy and confess my rebellion, I'd be shocked that not only had they *known* I had been in rebellion, but also they had *trusted God* enough to leave the work to Him. Now that's powerful and showed me even more vividly the reality of our faith.

I remember not long after Hans and I were married, Amy Grant came out with her song, "Just Like My Father's Eyes." I so understood that song and cherished those words, also wanting people to see the love of God in my eyes. Recently, I heard a wonderful message where the speaker asked us all to do something unusual. He asked us to picture in our minds the Lord's arms. He illustrated many ways we might picture them. Many would picture them closed in front in a position of retribution or disapproval. Some would picture them open in a welcoming way. My immediate picture to my surprise was of my *own father's arms* enfolded around me in a loving, safe, accepting, secure embrace. Wow! That's certainly a beautiful example of spiritual leadership that *works*. Though not perfect, it created in me an image of our Lord as a God of love as my own Heavenly Father who loves *me*...."just like my father's arms!"

Powerpoints

First, from the example of Donna's own father, here are some hints on how to be a good spiritual leader in your home:

❑ **Pray!** Above all, my dad is a man of prayer! He and Mom prayed for each one of us and our future mates even before our births. Every problem was prayed about, every need brought to God.

❑ **Listen!** From the time your children are young, give them your undivided attention. This should be on a regular basis so they feel you truly care. I still treasure the breakfasts "out with Daddy" I had with him alone, and I continue to enjoy those rare occasions we can be together.

❑ **Put your family first.** Learn how to set aside your work to leave it at the office to build a relationship with them. That will build important memories for each child.

❑ **Love them unconditionally.** Encourage your children to be who God wants them to be. Ask the Lord to show you the special needs of each child, and then be creative in leading them to grow.

❑ **Live what you believe!** That does not mean you have to be perfect. Just be willing to walk according to God's Word, and *ask* forgiveness from your kids or wife if you blow it by your words or actions. Then start over anew!

❑ **Seize the moment!** Make the time, and tune into those teachable moments with your kids. Share your heart! Be sure you *tell* your kids your testimony, and explain *why* you choose to do what you do (go to church, not go to certain places, etc.). Be sure to pray together with your kids about their problem or situation. And ask them to pray for you for specific needs or requests you have as well.

❑ **Take time <u>alone</u> with each child to focus on them.** Talk through with your spouse each of your visions of the needs and gifts of each child, and get alone with each one on a regular basis. Hans schedules one or two of his trips a year to include our children. He will be taking our twelve-year-old, Jeremy, with him to Brazil this summer.

We don't claim to have mastered the male spiritual leadership issue in our home. However, Donna and I have worked together to provide solutions so that we can attempt to raise our children in the right atmosphere. Some of the other practices that we follow, which we would pass on to you for your consideration, are:

1. For Fathers:

❑ Lower your expectations and do what you can do.

❑ Think bite-size pieces: Start with having family devotions, maybe just three times a week. Use a creative devotional book to help you, and pray together. Then come up with a list of annual minimal goals for what you would like to do with the children to provide spiritual influence.

❑ Be honest with your children about your struggles, and ask them for their input.

❑ Make this area a part of your accountability group.

❑ Beg, borrow, and steal any good ideas you can find from other fathers who seem to make this work.

2. For Mothers:

❑ Learn to back off. Work at allowing your husband the freedom and room to lead.

❑ Learn to back up. Pray for your husband, for the Lord to help him lead spiritually, and remember to support him when he does take the initiative.

❑ *When* you both fail, not *if* you fail, get back up and give it another try. Don't feel defeated. Starting over is always better than giving up.

FIVE

NEVER TRY TO WALK IN HER SHOES

Understanding the World of Your Wife

❑ Few men take the initiative to really walk in their wives' shoes even for a full day.

❑ Men and women have entirely different views of reality when it comes to those moments when he comes home from work in the evening.

❑ The best medicine I ever take to help me appreciate Donna's lot in life is to switch roles with her for a few days.

❑ Your understanding and compassion for her will grow proportionate to your seeing life from her point of view.

Jenny was newly married to a man nine years her senior. Their house had been his "bachelor pad." She made it into a nice home. She worked at a dentist's office and he as an accountant. When they conceived their first child, she worked part time until their son arrived. At that point life changed dramatically for Jenny! As many first-time moms do, she quit her job to be home full time with her son.

Now home full time, Jenny was lonely, tied down to the house, and busy trying to manage household demands along with a new baby. Tom continued his routine just as he always had, committed to all of his same outside activities. He continued to golf and take a couple nights a week for his bowling and weekends away fishing with the guys. Even after their second son arrived, he never even paused to consider what Jenny's life was like.

In spite of our more "liberated" age, many men live as Tom has. He assumes that as the provider, he is doing his part for his family. He wonders "what *does* Jenny *do* all day?" Tom never considers trying to walk in her shoes or even laying aside some of his "bachelor" habits. He has it great! At least according to him he does.

But what about Jenny? For a long time she carried on, did it all, and put up with all of his absence. Many women in her situation would have fallen into an affair or struggled along growing bitter at being misunderstood and forced to basically raise the children alone. Jenny, however, had come to faith in Christ through a local Bible study. She found friendship and encouragement from other young mothers. As she grew in the Lord, she not only tried to share Christ with Tom, but she also sought to grow closer to him in their marriage.

One of the best things Jenny did was to begin to *give* Tom more responsibility for their kids. She would set up occasional evenings to leave the kids with Tom and take the night off to enjoy an evening with friends. She would arrange baby-sitting so she and Tom could go out together. Jenny has found ways to adjust and grow, but still, overall, I'm sure she feels Tom doesn't truly appreciate her.

TOP TEN TIP

Reverse Roles Once a Year

From a Southern California Dad: "At least once a year I ask my wife to take off and go see her parents or spend the weekend with some of her girlfriends. And while she's gone, I try to take care of the home front as she likes so that she's not too discouraged at the mess she finds upon her return. This accomplishes two purposes in our marriage:

1. She gets her batteries recharged with some needed rest and a refreshing change of pace.

2. I get to be reminded what her life is like, which helps greatly when we live our normal roles and conflicts arise."

PULLING UP THE DRAWBRIDGE?

To contrast how men and women view those moments when they come home from work in the evening, listen to this humorous description by Jim Smith in his book, *Learning to Live with the One You Love:*

> The average man comes home believing that, having put in a hard day at work, it is now his God-given right to retire to his castle. He now wishes to enter his castle, pull up the drawbridge, and let the alligators swim in the moat. He is not particularly thrilled when he learns that there are some alligators loose in the castle.

> Now a woman's idea of an evening well spent is called "sharing"—in detail. The career woman wants to share her day with her husband—in detail—and the homemaker wants to share war stories from the home front. And what about the woman who has little children at home and has not been out of the house? She has been locked up with the "Viet Cong" all day and can't wait to turn them over to him the minute he walks in the door. She would like to have an adult conversation—in detail—with her husband (pp. 34–35).

Have you ever noticed that most men think they have spent a meaningful evening at home with their wives if they have simply been under the same roof? No conversation, no dialogue, no give and take, but they're there, in the same place at the same time—he thinks that means "closeness."

A man wants his wife to behave more or less like a good golden retriever, that is, she should come around occasionally and pass through the room, letting him acknowledge and pat her. Then she should go on doing whatever she was doing, come back in about an hour to let him pat and acknowledge her again. If she does that, he feels that he has spent a wonderful, warm evening with her. When she complains, "You never spend any time with me," he's shocked.

"What?" he yells. "I've been home all week." What he needs to understand is that, at least metaphorically, a woman is not a golden retriever, but more like a lap dog. She would like to have more closeness and intimacy.

A couple in Nebraska wrote us about their typical exchange in the evening after work (they both work outside the home): "I'll come home, and she'll ask me how my day went. I'm tired and ready for a change of pace—not wanting to talk about what I just left behind—so I'll answer with that great four-letter explanation that is good for almost any occasion, "fine." For a man this is a signal that he does not want to talk. But she is not satisfied. My friend goes on, "She wants more details. She wants to know what happened, what discussions I had today, what big decisions I made, what plans I made for our future. Although I know she is not asking for *every* detail of my day, I do find it exhausting to basically have to rehearse the whole day again. Perhaps I could record my day, and she could listen to the tape!"

> ### TOP TEN TIP
> *Ladies Night Out*
>
> From a wife living overseas:
>
> "Every so often Harold will take the kids for an evening and tell me to go out for dinner and a movie with my friends. *And*, he does not expect to be repaid in kind with his friends. That really means a lot to me."

This husband identified very succinctly the need a woman feels with her life mate—that need for intimate communication at the end of every day. Furthermore, my friend wrote this in our questionnaire about his wife's number one need: "I believe my wife's number one need is for me to communicate or talk *more* with her." Again the knowing is there, it is the energy that often fails.

OF NOBLE CHARACTER

Let's take a closer look at the life of a woman. And for a moment let's glimpse into Proverbs 31, where Scripture gives us the picture of "The Wife of Noble Character." This passage written centuries ago may seem at first pass totally detached from modern life in the '90s. But as with all of Scripture, there is a gold mine of wisdom and practical application if you look carefully:

A wife of noble character who can find? She is worth far more than rubies. Her husband has full confidence in her and lacks nothing of value. She brings him good, not harm, all the days of her life. She selects wool and flax and works with eager hands. She is like the merchant ships, bringing her food from afar. She gets up while it is still dark; she provides food for her family and portions for her servant girls. She considers a field and buys it; out of her earnings she plants a vineyard. She sets about her work vigorously; her arms are strong for her tasks. She sees that her trading is profitable, and her lamp does not go out at night. In her hand she holds the distaff and grasps the spindle with her fingers. She opens her arms to the poor and extends her hands to the needy. When it snows, she has no fear for her household; for all of them are clothed in scarlet. She makes coverings for her bed; she is clothed in fine linen and purple. Her husband is respected at the city gate, where he takes his seat among the elders of the land. She makes linen garments and sells them, and supplies the merchants with sashes. She is clothed with strength and dignity; she can laugh at the days to come. She speaks with wisdom, and faithful instruction is on her tongue. She watches over the affairs of her household and does not eat the bread of idleness. Her children arise and call her blessed; her husband also, and he praises her: "Many women do noble things, but you surpass them all." Charm is deceptive, and beauty is fleeting; but a woman who fears the *Lord* is to be praised. Give her the reward she has earned, and let her works bring her praise at the city gate. (Prov. 31:10-31)

For many women this picture is actually depressing. The qualities and gifts of this woman are praised and lifted up to be our goal to seek as wives and mothers. But how? But when? Is this what we women really even want today? I, Donna, remember how encouraging it was for me to learn that this woman was most likely at least in her fifties! It took time for her to develop the many areas of work and productiveness she is praised for. I do want her traits, but I don't know if I will reach them any time soon.

You may be a young woman with your first young child, or you may be the mother of many children of varying ages. Whether you are home full time, juggling part-time work, or a have full-time career, it is likely the bulk of home responsibility falls on your shoulders! Managing it all is overwhelming!

Men often don't truly understand all that is involved in homemaking. They take their wives for granted, knowingly or unknowingly. These husbands assume that their wives are just fine with the way things are. "Appreciation" and "gratefulness" are not two words that would come to mind for most men when they think of what their wives do to carry the load at home. But, men, that is what your wives need! Men usually assume that since they carry their workload without complaint, so should their wives. Right? *Wrong!*

When we go back to Ephesians 5:25, 28, and 33, we remember that the command to the husband is to *love* his wife. One of the most powerful ways to love her is to *show her you appreciate her and are deeply grateful for all she does each day.* In fact, Peter exhorts, "Husbands, in the same way *be considerate* as you live with your wives" (1 Peter 3:7). Why? Because God commands it? Yes! But also because of the *reward* you will receive by seeking to enter into her world.

RESPECT, RESPECT, RESPECT

A lot of us men get hung up trying to be control freaks. If we are in a position of leadership where we work or at least have control over our jobs, we tend to carry that tendency of control into our wife's domain. We must learn to respect her world and the decisions she makes about those things she is responsible for. In our home we try to practice the motto: "He who is in charge of the task gets to decide how it will be done."

One of our "wife" friends wrote this interesting story about a battle she faced in this arena having to do with washing the windows right before her parents came. I have never been able to appreciate the level of emotional intensity that rises in Donna whenever family are coming to town. As far as I'm concerned, life should just carry on as usual until we go pick them up at the airport to bring them home. Why can't they see us the way we live every day? This is no small source of irritation between us as Donna goes into "visitors are coming to town mode."

Our friend Sara told us this story:

> This past spring I decided that I wanted the windows washed badly enough to pay someone else to do it. My parents' imminent visit was part of the motivation. I knew just who to call, had already figured out a way to pay for it, and had placed the call. Unfortunately, the gentleman called back during dinner, and my husband answered the phone. Thinking it was a telemarketing sale, he said, "No, we don't need the windows cleaned. Thank you very much."
>
> "Honey," I exclaimed, "I called them. I want it done before Mom gets here."
>
> "We don't need to spend money on that. I'll do it, or the kids will." And so it went. You guessed it. Next week my parents came and went despite the dirty windows. The week after Paul went on a business trip, I cleaned the windows myself for "free."

And then Sara shared with us the punch line: When we asked the question, "If you could change anything about your husband, what would it be?" she answered, "Have him really trust my judgment in my areas of responsibility instead of second-guessing me." Respect is a two-way street, and we husbands must cut our wives the needed slack. It reminded us of one of our favorite sayings of late:

**Blessed are the control freaks
for they shall inhibit the earth.**

THE DEMANDING SCHEDULES OF WORK

Hans has always tried to listen when I tell him about the responsibilities I carry. Ever since we have had children (for fifteen years), *travel* has been a part of our lives. For the first few years, Hans traveled into Eastern Europe as part of our ministry of training pastors and Christian leaders. Then for the past several years, he's traveled as the director of our mission organization to our churches and mission fields around the world. Much of the time I have been home with our children, only occasionally traveling with Hans. By keeping our other priorities straight and making adjustments each year to the schedule to be sure we have adequate time for our marriage and family, we've done well overall. But when friction and stress start to show up, we are forced to take the time out to figure out what's gone wrong.

Through the years we have come to those times where I'm feeling discouraged by all of the various aspects of bearing the weight on the home front. We realize that the best means of *coping*, even better, doing my job well, is to have Hans' true understanding and support. As we talk it through, he comes to realize more how much I carry and do as a homemaker. The expectations and needs of the children, their schools, activities, carpool, our church, friends, and so on all weigh very heavily on the homemaker.

The intricacy of all of those demands and the "24-hour-a-day element" of it all sometimes add up to major overload for any woman. Add to those responsibilities the element of a husband away on travel or a job outside the home herself, and "Whew!" Most women say, "I've had it!" Sometimes when Hans has been on a heavy travel schedule, one more kid's asking me something or calling "Mom!" and I blurt out, "Hey, kids, that's it! I can't hear 'Mom' again. Just call 'Dad' (just so I can hear it), and I'll answer anyway."

So what is the key? How does the husband meet this need for understanding and relief in his wife? First, he must truly listen. Ask questions to dig deeper into her world. Then take action to bring her relief whenever he can. Men, sacrificial love is needed here in the down-to-earth nitty-gritty of life.

Try a few of these tips on for size:

WORKAHOLISM IS ANYTHING BUT HEALTHY

Recent studies show that one reason women always seem to outlive men is because of the stress men face in their careers. It seems that even women who hold high-pressured career jobs themselves don't internalize the work to the extent that we men do.

For males, it seems that the ego is all wrapped up in our work. Thus, the tendency is to become lost in the job and neglect the home front. The ironic thing here is that men would be far more healthy, balanced, and happy if they were more engaged in the domestic home side of their lives.

❑ Tell me how you are doing today.

❑ Have you had some "downtime" today?

❑ Come on, kids, let's go for a drive/walk/bike ride/so on.

❑ I'll do the dishes with the kids tonight. Thanks for the great dinner!

> ### TOP TEN TIP
> *Most Men Are Shocked at*
> *What They Find!*
>
> On those occasions when Hans has "walked in my shoes," truly carrying the responsibilities I normally carry for more than one day, he is always *shocked!* Most women feel that their husbands don't have a clue. And I must say, most husbands in America in the 1990s truly don't. I'm so grateful that Hans is willing to do that from time to time.
>   Give it a try, men. Walk in her shoes for a day or two. But watch out, for you may be in for a real surprise!

❑ I understand, your day would have certainly done *me* in! It means so much to me that you take such good care of our kids and our home. Thank you.

❑ Pick a night this week and go out for dinner with your friends. I'll cook dinner and take care of the kids.

❑ Let's go out for dinner alone—just you and me.

Whatever you do, men, find a way to give your wife true relief. Why? Partly because you are commanded to. Remember "Love" from Ephesians 5 and "Be Considerate" from 1 Peter 3. But beyond that you do it for the great reward of a *happy wife!* She is not going to "quit" her work. To the contrary, your true understanding will give her the joy of knowing you are truly carrying the weight with her. She'll have more joy and strength to continue each day.

Last year Hans decided to send me down to Phoenix each year for a getaway to be with my parents and have a break from my responsibilities. I had expressed to him a reality that had just dawned on me. The weight of home responsibility *never* truly shifts off of my shoulders!

Even when I'm able to go on a ministry trip with Hans or a getaway just for the two of us, the burden of childcare, meals, and so on still falls on me to arrange and carry in our absence.

On those occasions when Hans has "walked in my shoes," truly carrying the responsibilities I normally carry for more than one day, he is always *shocked!* Most women feel that their husbands don't have a clue. And I must say, most husbands in America in the 1990s truly don't. I'm so grateful that Hans is willing to "walk in my shoes" from time to time.

Just this last weekend Hans got a firsthand reminder of all that I do. I went to bed *all day*—just one day with a sinus infection. (Most of the time I just go on, but since I had been dizzy the night before, I decided to go to bed for just one day.) That night, Hans said, "I don't believe you do it!" After just one day of dealing with four kids, their friends, questions, spats, and trying to do some household jobs at the same time, he was overwhelmed. He told me to remind him of that day the next time he looked at me funny for the way I sometimes am at the end of a day of single responsibility for our family and household.

Men, loving your wife as Christ does the church sounds like an impossible standard to attain to. But the sacrifice Christ gave of laying aside His rights and privileges as the Son of God was much greater. He is not only your example, but He also has promised to give you His power to be what you should be as a husband!

HERO HUSBANDS WE KNOW

Not long ago we had the chance to have Christian singer Steve Green in our home for an evening. He was in town shooting a video for our ministry, and Donna and I wanted our kids to get a chance to get to know him personally. Because Steve grew up as one of our missionary kids in Argentina, we have known his family since before he was married. His parents Charles and Jo Green served with CBInternational for almost forty years in South America.

As our kids pumped Steve with questions that evening, he told us about the new travel bus he had built. Since he spends most of his life on the road, he has a big bus for his band and back-up crew. They also sleep in the bus while on the road. For several years Steve's wife, Mary Jean, and their two children traveled with him to all his concerts. They all lived together in their big bus. Sounds like one big happy family experience doesn't it? It was, but it didn't last. Life on the road gets old after a while, especially as the children get older and start school. Thus the need for a new bus and new strategy.

Now Steve Green travels without Mary Jean and the children to most of his concerts. But they are not neglected or forgotten. He has several special things he does to make them feel important, which will remain his private family secrets. The one expression of love and understanding he practices consistently for Mary Jean is something that everyone who goes to his concerts knows of. In the middle of his evening program, invariably he will pick up a stage phone and talk with his wife and children live on-stage. Her voice is piped through to the audience so everyone can hear her voice and receive greetings from Mary Jean. While they are talking, either a video or still photos of her and the children are displayed on the large stage screen.

What is Steve communicating by all this fuss? A mountain of good will. He is letting his wife know that he is thinking about her while he is away. And he is telling her that she is important enough to him that he wants all his concert goers to know her too—*he is not the only important member of the Green family*. Finally, he is making a strong statement to the world that he is a deeply committed family man and hopelessly in love with his wife. That is good protection for a life on the road!

Powerpoints

The biggest surprise, husbands, is how relatively little it will take for you to do this for your wife. Your volunteering in things like—"kicking her out of the kitchen" will go *far* to show her you care. Make these acts as spontaneous as possible, or choose a day or two each week when you actually sign up for regular domestic duties. Simple action along with your hugs and caring about her world will usually be *all she needs* to jump back into the "fray." Although she may still be tired, her spirits will be lifted and more ready to "charge" into her life's demands.

Here are a few suggestions, expanding our previous list with more suggestions:

❑ When you come home, try asking her, "Tell me how you are doing today?"

❑ Ask her, "Have you had some 'downtime' today?"

❑ Try this with the children, "Come on, kids, let's go for a drive/walk/bike ride/shopping/errands and so on."

❑ "I'll do the dishes with the kids tonight. Thanks for the great dinner!"

❑ Shower her with words of appreciation, like "I understand, your day would have certainly done me in! It means so much to me that you take such good care of our kids and our home. Thank you."

❑ Give her that night out: "Pick a night this week and go out for dinner with your friends. I'll cook and take care of the kids."

❑ If she seems exhausted, irritable, and hostile, *take action.* Tell her you'll be in charge for forty-five minutes or longer so she can retreat to a private room to read or have a few moments of quiet.

For the many men who travel, there is special advice for you, before you take off and after you land from your latest business trip. Travel away from home adds unique pressure to a marriage, to the husband-wife relationship, and to the role of a father with his children. Some important tips to remember along the way are these:

1. Before you leave

❑ Make sure the family is taken care of. Leave your wife a detailed schedule of where you will be, what you will be doing, and how you can be reached.

❑ Spend extra quality time with your wife and children before departure.

❑ Don't expect a hit-and-run relationship prior to your departure to satisfy your sexual needs.

2. While you are on the road

❑ Be sure to call your family regularly.

❑ If your wife or family feels they need it, carry a beeper along.

❑ Leave love notes behind for your wife and family to find.

❑ Send mail to your family if you are gone for a longer period of time.

❑ Send gifts or flowers if it is an extended trip.

3. Take care of yourself while you are traveling

❑ Try to maintain consistency in your quiet time.

❑ Avoid temptation at any cost.

❑ Try not to spend too much time alone.

4. Upon reentry

❑ Don't go straight back to work if you can help it. Your family needs you first.

❑ Plan some travel-recovery time.

❑ Work aggressively to debrief your wife on your travels.

❑ Do the same with your children.

❏ Don't try to cover travel guilt by showering your family with pre-
sents—what they need is some quality time with you.

Six

It's a Man's World

Respect for the Dignity of Your Woman's Worth

❑ It has been decades since "Leave It to Beaver," but many men in the '90s are still hung up on the old traditional role of the husband and wife portrayed in the '50s.

❑ Even when women earn more, men rarely contribute their share at home—a major source of tension in the modern marriage.

❑ If a man's home is "his castle," he needs to treat his spouse as the *queen*, not the *maidservant!*

Even though it has been decades since "Leave It to Beaver," many men in the '90s are still hung up on the old traditional view of the worth of the husband and wife. Many of us grew up with the television models of "Ozzie and Harriet," "Father Knows Best," "Leave It to Beaver," "The Dick Van Dyke Show," and "I Love Lucy." In all of those cases, Mom was the faithful homemaker while Dad did all of the "important work" outside of the home. Mom took care of the kids, took care of the dishes, and took care of the house, while Dad was out there bringing home the paycheck and making a mark on the world.

The subtle undertone and attitude that was projected through all of those role models was that *Dad's world was more important than Mom's*—at least what he did was more important than what she did. Of course, we find that today the entertainment media portrays a much different image, some of it positive and leaning much more to the biblical model of dignity and respect for the woman.

We have to come back again to the beautiful model of Proverbs 31 to see how absolutely worthwhile the woman is as a partner in a marriage. What she does is full of dignity, honor, and worthy of full respect:

A Woman's Worth
Proverbs 31:10–11
A wife of noble character who can find? She is worth far more than rubies. Her husband has full confidence in her and lacks nothing of <u>value</u>.

In our early years of marriage, I expected Donna to play the good housewife and servant role that my own mother played in our home. And I have to confess that I thought it was much more important that I receive an education for my profession than it was for Donna. Today I regret that we did not allow her more freedom in the early years to pursue her educational objectives before the children came. Not that she is complaining because she loves the role she has as a wife, mother, and homemaker. In addition to her role in the home, she has a fulfilling ministry with women in our church. But she also has worked outside of the home. This professional side to her has also given her a great deal of satisfaction and sense of worth.

WE'VE COME A LONG WAY—MAYBE

This is not the 1950s

Many of us grew up with the television models of "Ozzie and Harriet," "Father Knows Best," "Leave It to Beaver," "The Dick Van Dyke Show," and "I Love Lucy." In all of those cases, Mom was the faithful homemaker while Dad did all of the "important work" outside of the home.

This picture of the '50s is hardly a working model for the '90s. Aside from being impractical, it's really not all that biblical.

In the last chapter we looked at the need for a man to understand the *work* of his wife: her *role*. This chapter is about her *worth*. The extreme that the world projects to us is that a woman should get out of the home if she is going to do anything important. The working world has opened up to the woman, and we've seen some of those "glass ceilings" shatter everywhere. We applaud this greater opportunity for women outside of the home, but that's not the full picture. Can a woman fulfill a role of worthiness, dignity, and respect by what she does inside the home as a homemaker, wife, and mother? We would say the answer is a resounding yes! There is nothing wrong and a lot right with wanting to fill that role. And, in fact, the trend is that more and more women are leaving the workplace and their careers to go back to a simpler life of more quality and value in the home during the child-raising years of their marriages.

Recent surveys and studies are showing that the career model for the working mother is not all that it was cracked up to be. Just as more and more families are moving back to their roots in the hometowns they grew up in, looking for a simpler life of more quality and a slower pace, women are leaving the corporate world to go back home in great numbers in the '90s. Financial realities, of course, demand that some mothers work. Whether the wife in your home is a homemaker or employed outside the home, the husband must learn to appreciate her worth.

How do we handle our roles in the Finzel household? I, Hans, have grown to appreciate more and more, as the years have gone by, the incredible value that Donna provides in our home and marital relationship. I appreciate that she is home raising our children, and we work hard to try to keep it that way. As far as I'm concerned, what she does is just as important and valuable as what I do. She has chosen to be in the home to pour her life into our four young children and to prepare them to be men and women of God as they enter adulthood and go into the world. The bottom line from my viewpoint is this: *What she does is as important as what I do!* I try to show her this every week and every month in the following ways:

❑ By listening to what is going on in her life.

❑ By dropping what I have to do to help her with what she needs to do when she asks.

❑ By honoring her publicly whenever I have an opportunity to do so.

❑ By communicating to our children the valuable role she plays in our home and family.

❑ By allowing her great freedom in the decision-making areas that affect her responsibilities in our family.

❑ By seeking to provide "vacation" away from her job just as I get vacation away from my work.

THE VIEW FROM HER SIDE

Let's take a moment to hear how Donna feels about her role in our home: Life as a full-time homemaker with four kids in the 1990s is a huge challenge. Life in America with all of our modern conveniences has accelerated the pace and expectations put upon the family. Choices bombard us constantly. Somehow this has seemed to isolate us from one another within the family, church, and community, as our lives are so busy and full. I especially remember when we first arrived back in America after living overseas for nearly ten years, how shocking it all was. We would watch in amazement at how everyone lived and wondered, "Where *are* they all going? What is all the great *hurry* about?" We soon discovered that much of the energy and time expended by people involved:

- ❑ **"doing"**—activities such as soccer, ice skating, baseball, football, ballet, and church clubs.

- ❑ **"going"**—to pull off all of those activities, the family van had almost become "home."

- ❑ **"getting"**—shopping and consuming is truly an American art form. Nowhere else in the world has all of the options and availability or commercialism to draw people to buy, buy, buy.

As the homemaker, together with Hans, we've sought to find our own way, as I know many of you have, to *not* be ruled by the standard "way it is" described above. We seek to make our family life, relationships with our kids, and ministry for our Lord our primary focus and motivation. I believe we do have a very close bond as a family, and we spend a lot of time at home together. Inviting the kids' friends in and opening our home inviting others in are things we're doing more and more.

> **We want to make "being"**
> —*a close family*
> —*more like our Lord Jesus Christ*
> —*a caring family for others in our neighborhood*
>   *and church family*
> —*a loving testimony of a Christian family*
> **the priority in our lives.**

Yes, I do find joy in my role as a homemaker. As long as I maintain balance and make choices based upon our true priorities as much as possible, our home is peaceful and a great place to be in. Sometimes, though, reality demands that our schedule be too full, and priorities are left in the dust as I run about doing, going, and getting! That's life, and no home is perfect. When I get discouraged and feel overwhelmed wanting to give up, usually it means I've been doing, going, and getting too much. This *is* a huge job. But it is rewarding to know that I personally have the daily opportunity to be with my kids in their formative years, to convey our values, and to guide them.

Taking care of the children and teaching them responsibility go hand in hand. A great help when I get those feelings that "this is a thankless job" comes from the promise the Lord has given to us:

> Whatever you do, work at it with all your heart, as working for the Lord, not for men, since you know that you will receive an inheritance from the Lord as a reward. It is the Lord Christ you are serving.
> —Col. 3:23-24

Men, learn to respect the role your wife plays in your marriage and family. If she works outside the home, then you and she need to be equal partners in fulfilling all of the domestic duties that you face in the home. It's not fair for her to have to work just as much as you do and then have to carry the entire load of the household when you both get home in the evening. That is a no-brainer. And yet we are amazed at how many men still feel that their wives should be super-women who can do it all.

MEN: ACTIVELY FOCUS ON HER WORTH

Whether or not they were employed outside the home, nine out of ten women surveyed by the Families and Work Institute said it was their responsibility to take care of their families. And according to another recent study, women who *outearn* their husbands do even *more* housework by a large margin than women who make about the same as their husbands:

Even when women earn more, men rarely contribute their share at home—another major source of tension. When any of her three children gets sick, Lisa, a pathologist, is the one who takes a day off—even though her husband, George, a computer programmer, earns a third of what she does. "All of a sudden my work is secondary," she says (*Good Housekeeping*, January 1996, pp. 94–95).

If you find yourselves in the more traditional role of the husband working outside of the home and the wife working in the home, then you may need to learn to respect and give great dignity to what your wife does in the raising of your children and the care of your castle. If a man's home is "his castle," he needs to treat his spouse as the queen, not the maidservant!

I must keep reminding myself that God designed couples to be different for the very sake of providing color in the lifelong relationship we call marriage. Looking at myself as a husband, I know I haven't always made Donna's role a joyful one. But I'm learning, and I consciously consider her schedule and the demands upon her time as we go throughout our weekly routines. I try to give her plenty of notice on upcoming travel commitments and appointments, and try never to "spring" surprises on her that she can't prepare for! By doing that, I am showing respect for her role and contribution to our family. That has made life for Donna more fulfilling and has helped things run more smoothly overall in our home life.

TWO EXTREMES IN THE VIEWS OF A WOMAN'S ROLE

Whenever we think of the role of a woman, two extremes seem to drive us. First, there is the overly aggressive woman, who hates terms like "submission," or "that's the woman's place." It is difficult for this woman to be led by anyone, especially men. Second, there is the woman who lacks confidence to assert herself anywhere outside of the home. Even in the home, she views herself as personal servant to the demands of her husband.

Neither of these extremes is a biblical view of marriage. A survey of Scripture dealing with women paints an entirely different picture, most notably portrayed in the truths of Proverbs 31, which we have already begun to describe.

As a husband, I would challenge you to read through this "paraphrase" of Proverbs 31, and circle the qualities you see in your wife. Then share with her those good qualities you see in her, "praising her" by thanking her for the initiative she takes in meeting the needs of you and the kids in those areas. Remember, the woman portrayed here most certainly grew into being the "Noble Wife" over a period of years and received much praise from her husband along the way!

Proverbs 31—A Personal Paraphrase

The "wife of noble character" is said to be rare indeed! She is of highest value and worth, and her husband totally trusts her, not second-guessing her, but rather relying on her, knowing her work will bring him good, not harm, ALL THE DAYS OF HER LIFE. She is a woman with multiple skills and training, involved in commerce. She works very hard, even having her own income. She is strong, compassionate, generous, given to hospitality. She plans ahead and dresses herself and her family well. She decorates her home beautifully. She exudes "strength" and "dignity," but has a sense of humor. She speaks wisely and chooses her words carefully as she instructs her children. Her husband is respected highly. Her children and husband praise her. But her highest praise is that her beauty is inward as she is a great woman of God who walks closely to Him!

DOORMAT OR DIGNITY?

We appreciate Charles Swindoll's wrestling with the extremes of the "overly aggressive" versus the "doormat" type view of women in his booklet titled: *Woman: A Person of Worth and Dignity*. As he looks at the two extremes we just described, he carefully identifies the causes for these biblically inaccurate viewpoints:

1. A misunderstanding and mis-application of "submission."

Husbands and wives alike have done this. Pastors and other so-called authorities have also contributed to this most unfortunate problem.

2. A failure on the part of Christian husbands to carry out three essential responsibilities, namely:

> to think biblically
> to lead fairly
> to release unselfishly

3. A strong, well-organized action from the secular world system to "liberate" today's woman . . . regardless.

HER WORTH AND DIGNITY

"Frankly, I am convinced this underscores the fact that God never intended the woman to feel inferior or to live fearfully beneath some heavy cloud of unfair domination. While no one who takes Scripture seriously can deny that a wife must, indeed, fit into her husband's plans (1 Peter 3:1) and ultimately allow him the place of final authority in the home (Eph. 5:22), in no way is she ever viewed as an individual lacking in worth or dignity."

—Charles R. Swindoll

Even those who don't want to be "liberated" are made to appear foolish and backward. The happy homemaker, the fulfilled woman who enjoys being at home, is mocked by the system.

4. An equally strong resistance from some voices in Christendom to keep the Christian woman boxed in, seated, and silent.

Frankly, I am convinced this underscores the fact that God never intended the woman to feel inferior or to live fearfully beneath some heavy cloud of unfair domination. While no one who takes Scripture seriously can deny that a wife must, indeed, fit into her husband's plans (1 Peter 3:1) and ultimately allow him the place of final authority in the home (Eph. 5:22), in no way is she ever viewed as an individual lacking in worth or dignity (*Woman: A Person of Worth and Dignity*, Charles Swindoll, pp.8–9).

HERO HUSBANDS WE KNOW

I, Hans, just returned from an encouraging trip to meet with an acquaintance we'll call William, a hero of a husband, who lives in the beautiful rolling hills of eastern Pennsylvania. Fortunately also I had the chance to meet his lovely wife, Barb, and learn of their special relationship as it involves his respect for her role in their marriage.

William has been the president of an international ministry for twenty-five years. Four years ago they moved their world headquarters from New Jersey to Pennsylvania. During the process of renovating their new ministry center, they added 35,000 square feet of new offices to their complex. When it came time to work on interior design, his gifted wife, Barb, volunteered to take care of all planning for the furnishings, colors, wall coverings, paintings, and decorations. Quite a big job and big commitment for his spouse! William had two choices—bring in a "professional" and pay the big bucks or take a risk and allow Barb to use her gifts in his world.

Not every woman is gifted in interior decorating, but Barb is. I spent two days at their headquarters, and I can tell you that it is beautiful beyond description. Tastefully and professionally done, Barb left her mark on the world where her husband rules as chief executive. William's decision to let Barb come into his world in such a significant way communicates several important things.

❑ He trusts Barb.

❑ He believes that she can make significant contributions to his world.

❑ He views his wife as a partner in his work.

❑ He wants his wife to be connected to his world.

❑ He wants the other women at the office to see how involved he is with his spouse.

❑ He believes that she has much to offer him.

Many men are overprotective of their workplace, and they would just as soon their wives stayed away. Work is work and home is home, and never the two should meet. This unhealthy attitude builds barriers between a husband and a wife and makes her feel that his world is much more important than hers. Remember, he comes in and out of her life freely on the home front. Why can't she be a vital part of his world as well?

Powerpoints

The applications of this chapter have to do with men recognizing the worth of their wives, no matter what their role in life is. Whether she is a working career woman or a dedicated homemaker, there are things husbands can do to enhance her worth.

This is an assignment for husbands:

❑ *Try the yellow-pad approach:* If for some reason your wife was permanently taken out of your life tomorrow, what are all the things you would miss about her? Make a detailed list and write it down on a yellow pad.

❑ *Take a Proverbs 31 inventory:* Read carefully through Proverbs 31, and write down a list of all the valuable traits of the woman described. It would be especially helpful to read through the "paraphrase" found earlier in the chapter and circle the qualities you see in your wife. Then share with her those good qualities you see in her, "praising her" by thanking her for the initiative she takes in meeting your and the kids' needs in those areas.

❑ *Bring your wife into your life:* How much is your spouse involved in knowing about your world? Do you communicate that it is too complex for her to understand? Take the time and energy to let her in.

❑ *View your marriage as a partnership:* Since some guys still don't get it, or don't *want* to get it, work at this no-brainer. If she works outside the home, then you and she need to be equal partners in fulfilling all of the domestic duties that you face in the home. It's not fair for her to have to work just as much as you do and then have to carry the entire load of the household when you both get home in the evening.

❑ *Keep surprises to a minimum:* One way to show your respect for your marriage partner is to keep her well informed of all plans that you are making that affect her or the family. Do not spring business trips, outings with the guys, or vacation plans on her unannounced.

❑ *Discover her personal goals:* Talk to your wife about her long-range goals. Do you even know what her private aspirations are? Many husbands have no clue what the secret dreams of their wives are. If she has worth to you, then take the time to draw those dreams out of her.

❑ *Help her dreams happen:* Most women have dreams of being more than they are and doing something special with their lives. Help your wife reach those dreams by taking a submissive approach to her needs, in this case you as the man submitting to her in the spirit of Ephesians 5:21:

"Submit to one another out of reverence for Christ." Give up some of your personal goals and pursuits to allow her time to pursue hers.

❑ *Show her you value her in the little daily things of life:* We will repeat here the list found earlier in the chapter that Hans works on consistently in our home:

> By listening to what is going on in her life.
>
> By dropping what I have to do to help her with what she needs to do when she asks.
>
> By honoring her publicly whenever I have an opportunity to do so.
>
> By communicating to our children the valuable role she plays in our home and family.

> ### HIGHEST VALUE AND WORTH
>
> The "wife of noble character" is said to be rare indeed! She is of highest value and worth, and her husband totally trusts her, not second-guessing her, but rather relying on her, knowing her work will bring him good, not harm, ALL THE DAYS OF HER LIFE.
>
> A Proverbs 31 paraphrase

By allowing her great freedom in the decision-making areas that affect her responsibilities in our family.

By seeking to provide "vacation" away from her job just as I get vacation away from my work.

S E V E N
MISSING HER RADAR SIGNALS
Sensitivity to Her Needs and Your Listening Skills

❏ "Men think vertically. Men want women to get
   on with their lives, so that they can go back to
   watching 'Combat' reruns."—Tim Allen

❏ Something about tears always seems to get a
   man's attention.

❏ She doesn't want me to give her a quick, five-
   minute solution with ten easy steps to put this
   problem behind her. She needs me to listen to
   her, to know I care, to feel her hurt, and to sense
   her pain. Being a bottom-line, let's-fix-the-
   problem kind of guy, just sitting and listening is a
   big stretch.

❏ There is still no substitute for quiet, prolonged
   exposure of one soul to another.

A couple of summers ago we were tooling down the freeways of "Big Sky" Wyoming, enjoying a blissful family vacation get-away. The four children were happily playing in the back as Donna sat next to me in the copilot's chair of our family motor home. The only thing wrong with the picture that day was that my radar antenna was shut down.

Family vacations are always a great time for the Finzels. Donna especially looks forward to the hours that we will have alone sitting in the pilot and copilot seats of our traveling home-away-from-home. For her, it is a time to really debrief on a deeper level about everything that has been going on in both of our lives since the last time we went camping.

Unfortunately, for most of the men I know, they just seem to want to sit quietly and vegetate when they are driving down the freeway. In fact, I'm amazed at how many other couples have the same experience we do. The woman just can't understand why the man doesn't want to talk when they're finally alone. The man, on the other hand, finds his relaxation by just driving down the road endlessly, hour after hour, with only an occasional grunt of "yes" or "no."

I, Hans, personally find that one of the most relaxing things I can do is to just drive and be alone with my thoughts. Of course, I admit that I am not an avid conversationalist like some of my male friends. I'm sure there are some husbands who love to chatter as they tool down the freeways, but more often than not there is a communications chal-lenge. You would think that when a husband and wife are finally together with uninterrupted hours before them, the words would just begin to flow. But that's really not the case. One of the great chal-lenges is to break the log jams, clear the sludge out of the pipes, and get the words flowing between husband and wife.

SUMMER VACATIONS

One of the great challenges of summer vacation is to break the log jams, clear the sludge out of the pipes, and get the words flowing between hus-band and wife.

On this particular day, as we were enjoying the breathtaking beauty of the "Big Sky" country of Wyoming, stretching out endlessly toward the horizon, Donna was becoming more and more exasperated by my lack of communication. I think if she would have had access to a large 2x4, she probably would have pelted me on the head with it to get my attention. Finally, she broke into tears, which . . . yes, you guessed it . . . is much more effective than a 2x4! Women's tears do that to men.

What is it about tears that always seems to get a man's attention? As soon as I saw the tears begin to flow, I said to myself, "Oh! This is actu-ally serious stuff to her." I can't even believe how hardhearted and insen-sitive I am sometimes to tune out her needs. Donna began to pour out her heart to me about how difficult the last months had been as I was gone so much in my travels, and she was left home alone to fend for herself with all the responsibilities of the home and the four children.

"I've reached the limit, the edge . . . I mean it," she sobbed. "Something's got to give. I don't know what's over that edge, but I *know* it's not good! I just can't go on with our life this way." What followed was a long, long conversation about the cumulative effect on her of bearing the weight of our home life as I travel. We dug into her needs and my role in helping to take care of them. We discussed options and mostly I just listened to her talk. A man's response is always to try to fix the problem, but I bit my lip, kept my mouth shut, and tried to listen intensely as she poured out her heart to me.

One thing I learned in the process was that it is exactly the *process of pouring out her heart* that is extremely important to a woman. She doesn't want me to give her a quick, five-minute solution with ten easy steps to put this problem behind us. She needs me to listen to her, to know I care, to feel her hurt, and to sense her pain. Being

> ## TOP TEN TIP
> *Just Shut Up and Listen*
>
> "A man's response is always to try to fix the problem, but I bit my lip, kept my mouth shut, and tried to listen intensely as she poured out her heart to me."

a bottom-line, let's-fix-the-problem kind of guy, just sitting and listening is a big stretch for me.

That talk where she finally got through to me was the beginning of a healing moment and a healing time for us. In the subsequent months I began to take concrete steps to change my schedule and my approach to traveling since I realized the unusual pressure it placed on her. I consider Donna a superwoman, but no one can be all things to all men. Our hearts go out to the many single parents out there, who literally do have to be everything to the children they raise while they are trying to bring home a paycheck and make ends meet.

ON LISTENING AND OTHER
RARE EXOTIC HABITS

All of us task-oriented, obsessive-compulsive males must learn to slow down and let people into our lives. It may be popular in the 1990s to be a fast-tracker with a full daytimer, but we will impact people spiritually and permanently only by that one-on-one contact that can't be substituted. In this age of telecommunications and teleconnecting, *there is still no substitute for quiet, prolonged exposure of one soul to another.* With all the marvels of the Internet and a reach-out-and-touch-someone technology, husband and wife are more in need of quiet and prolonged communication than ever before. The more the craziness, the more communication protects the marriage.

I, Hans, am a full-blooded German. Therefore, I tend to be *task-oriented* by nature. Since I find myself in roles of leadership, I often think about how my Germanness affects my leadership relationships. Is it an unfair generalization to say that Germans are all task-oriented? Well, think about any Germans whom you know. Do they tend to be perfectionists, workaholics who rarely relax, and generally rigid in relationships? Probably. Sure, there are exceptions, but not among the many Germans I've known!

My beautiful, relationally oriented wife is always calling out to me, *"Hans, stop! Can't you just sit down for an hour and do nothing? Could we just talk?"* That is extremely hard for me to do ... to do "nothing." I guess deep down in my task-oriented nature, I see talking as not really accomplishing all that much. I tend to be an impatient conversationalist; that is, unless I am in a deep discussion that is driving me toward the accomplishment of another task, or unless I am in a situation where I can not get to my work and have some down time. Even when we go camping, I tend to spend my time tinkering with the equipment instead of just vegetating—which I think someone told me was the actual goal of this exercise. I have made good progress in recent years in learning to slow down, and most of that is due to Donna's positive influence on me.

When I talk to other men about this common ailment of obsessive behavior, they all seem to have the same problem—that is, their wives don't feel like they take enough time to listen. Tim Allen of "Home Improvement" fame summarizes it well:

> Men don't listen, particularly to women. This shouldn't be a big surprise. A woman will talk and talk and talk about some problem until a man cuts her off and says, "Here's what I'd do." Men are always giving advice out of their own experience. Men think vertically. Some guy is always bigger, badder, better. His car is nicer, his job more lucrative, his women prettier. Men live to vanquish those challenges. They don't mind helping a woman overcome her problems, if only she'll listen. Men want women to get on with their lives, so that they can go back to watching "Combat" reruns (*Don't Stand Too Close to a Naked Man*, Tim Allen, p. 210).

Well, I, Donna, am here to share the news with all you men out there who care to listen up. The news flash is this: *Women don't want to hear your advice!* They don't want solutions to their crises. They just want an arm around their shoulders and a soft-spoken, "I understand" (if you do!) or "I hear you, and I care about how you're feeling" (if you don't!).

They want to:

❏ SEE you care by your interest

❏ FEEL your closeness and love

❏ KNOW you have truly heard them

Just to make sure it is getting through to you, I'm going to say it one more time:

Women don't want to hear your advice!

In chapter 2 we briefly mentioned 1 Peter 3, where Peter spoke of the responsibilities of husbands and wives. So many times the subject of submission is the focus of teaching from this passage. As I, Donna, studied this passage for teaching last year, I was amazed to learn new meaning in these verses. Verse 7 reads, *Husbands, in the same way be considerate as you live with your wives, and treat them with respect as the weaker partner and as heirs with you of the gracious gift of life, so that nothing will hinder your prayers.* The words normally translated "weaker vessel" or "weaker partner" can also be translated literally, "feminine one." Our uniqueness as women is clear in this passage. Peter knew that, and he wrote clearly here God's command that husbands:

❑ Be considerate living with your wife

❑ Treat her with respect

❑ Understand her unique feminine needs

❑ Remember she is your coheir of salvation

If husbands fail to do those things, Peter said that their prayers will be hindered. That's powerful! Here we see again the foundation of all we want to convey in this book. If husbands will truly love their wives in this way, we believe their marriages and home life will be revolutionized.

At the top of the list of "feminine ways" is the woman's basic need for *affection.* In response to our very nonscientific survey of married couples, this need came through both as the number one need of women *and* as the one most husbands fail to meet in their wives. Let's repeat that here since we're talking about communication skills and a husband's need to listen to the needs of his wife:

**At the top of the list of "feminine ways"
is the woman's basic need for AFFECTION.**

In his book, *Learning to Live with the One You Love,* Jim Smith reveals that women have a desperate need for closeness—to be connected in their relationship with their husbands. Men, to the contrary, fear closeness, and actually feel safer with distance. Obviously, this creates barriers to affection (closeness) in husbands. Ironically, one of men's greatest needs—in the area of sexual satisfaction—won't usually be responded to by his wife if she doesn't first *feel close* to him!

LISTENING CAREFULLY TO HER INTIMATE NEEDS

We hesitated to write this book because of the flood of books already on the market in the area of Christian marriage. Who needs another book on marriage anyway? However, we were finally convinced to write the book by taking this unique approach of looking at, most specifically, how the husband can do a better job of living his role and fulfilling his responsibilities. Men, if you're reading this, at the top of your list of responsibilities is *"Learn to tune in to her radar signals."*

As we briefly mentioned in chapter 2, of all the books we have read on marriage, without a doubt our number one favorite is *His Needs, Her Needs: Building an Affair Proof Marriage* by Dr. William F. Harley, Jr. Nothing has helped us more in our own marriage. William Harley's underlying philosophy of a good marriage is simple and profound:

**"Become aware of each other's needs
and learn to meet them."**

It seems simple enough, but very, very hard to do on a consistent basis. You have to want to make your marriage work to get started down this road. We have appreciated Dr. Harley's work so much because he has helped us in our marriage identify what are the basic needs that each of us have and how different the needs of a man and a woman are. Even though we have some underlying similarities, we also have some dramatic differences in what we need to be happy in marriage. Dr. Harley goes on to state,

> When a man and woman marry, they share high expectations. They commit themselves to meeting certain intense and intimate needs in each other on an exclusive basis. Each agrees to "forsake all others," giving each other the exclusive right to meet these intimate needs. That does not imply that all needs are to be met by a spouse, but there are a few basic needs that most of us strictly reserve for the marriage bond. Most people expect their spouses to meet these special needs, since they have agreed not to allow anyone else to meet them (*His Needs, Her Needs*, William F. Harley, Jr., pp. 9–10).

Some of you may think that Dr. Harley's list is simplistic, but in our survey of many married couples, we find an amazing similarity. Here again are the two sets of five categories that have consistently surfaced as the basic needs of a man and a woman in marriage:

The man's five most basic needs in marriage are:

1. Sexual fulfillment
2. Recreational companionship
3. Attractive spouse
4. Domestic support
5. Admiration

The woman's five most basic needs in marriage are:

1. Affection
2. Conversation
3. Honesty and openness

4. Financial support

5. Family commitment

What happens when these needs are not met? Well, many things happen, ranging from mild dissatisfaction at one end of the continuum all the way to affairs and possibly divorce at the other end. One thing is for sure, a marriage where the needs are not being met will be an unhappy one. Somehow the spouses will look elsewhere to get those needs met and/or remain in great misery, loneliness, and isolation with unfulfilled needs. Dr. Harley goes on to give us this sober warning:

> In marriages that fail to meet those needs, I have seen, strikingly and alarmingly, how consistently married people choose the same pattern to satisfy their unmet needs: the extramarital affair. People wander into affairs with astonishing regularity, in spite of whatever strong, moral or religious convictions they may hold. Why? Once a spouse lacks fulfillment in any of the five needs, it creates a thirst that must be quenched. If changes do not take place within the marriage to care for that need, the individual will face the powerful temptation to fill it outside of marriage.
>
> In order to make our marriages affair proof, we cannot hide our heads in the sand. The spouse who believes his or her partner is "different," and despite unmet needs, would never take part in an affair, may receive a devastating shock some day. Instead, we need to understand the warning signs that an affair could happen, how such liaisons may begin, and how to strengthen the weak areas of a marriage in the face of such a relationship (*His Needs, Her Needs*, William F. Harley, Jr., pp. 9–11).

Some of you who are reading these words have a marriage that has already gone down this road of extramarital affairs. It has destroyed your faith; it has wounded you; and it has created great barriers between the two of you. Please consider the help that Dr. Harley can offer, and believe that healing and restoration is possible. We have several dear friends—married couples—who have gone down this road of affairs to the edge of the cliff of divorce and come back to survive and rebuild a trusting, fulfilling marriage. It can be done if there is a commitment on both of your parts to learn your love languages and how to meet each other's needs.

How Close Do You Want to Be?

A Harvard University research project brought out some startling differences as observed in young boys and girls at play. The girls' games were always shorter than the boys' games. They also noticed that the little boys preferred games with lots of rules. The boys appeared to have about as much fun discussing infractions of the rules as they did actually playing the game. In the little girls' games, if there was a quarrel, the girls were more likely to end the game rather than risk a fracture in the relationship. The girls apparently felt that *relationships* were more important than *rules*.

> ### TOP TEN TIP
> *Let Her Let Go of It*
>
> "When women talk something out in detail, somewhere along the line they let go of it. But unless they do this, they keep holding on."
>
> —Dr. Jim Smith
> *Learning to Live with the One You Love*

There is some humor in this when you look at it objectively, but in reality there is often much pain, feelings of rejection, and growing distance in a marriage in which the couple fails to understand and meet the needs of their spouse.

Early in our marriage I couldn't understand myself well enough to explain why I did not feel close to Hans when all seemed to be well between us. Sometimes for no apparent reason, when Hans would be ready and interested, I just could *not* consider our having sexual intimacy. Usually, we'd go for a walk or just talk it out, and then feelings of distance would surface in me. As I shared and Hans listened, issues sometimes large, but usually small (yet undealt with), often would surface. As I "off-loaded" those issues and listened to Hans' feedback, his caring and listening were key to restoring in me a sense of intimacy. As a woman, I needed him to know my thoughts and feelings, and I needed to know his. I needed for him to just *want* to be with me and listen, hold hands, hug, and *be close.* A woman needs to talk it out and "let go" in order to be finished with a given topic before she can move on emotionally.

Dr. Jim Smith reveals his insights on this reality:

> When women talk something out in detail, somewhere along the line they let go of it. But unless they do this, they keep holding on. Any man who doesn't grasp that is doomed to keep on hitting the same communication wall over and over again. I can tell you that it took me only twenty years to learn this about my wife. Since then I've observed it in most women. There's something that happens in women that doesn't go on in men.
>
> The husband says, "Let's drop it. Let it alone. We've already hacked that thing to pieces." But the wife doesn't see it that way. And if hubby doesn't let her discuss it and clear the air, it will come up again!
>
> That reminds me of the man who said, "When my wife and I get into an argument, she gets historical!"

CAN CHILDREN GET IN THE WAY?

As our children started to arrive, it became more and more difficult to steal the time to maintain our closeness. We tell every young couple that is expecting their first child the same warning: *Adjusting to having a child is many times more difficult than adjusting to marriage.* The couple without a child can live a pretty self-centered life, but that first baby will knock the selfishness right out of you both. At least we hope that the father is there to do his share. As my father told me upon the arrival of our first child, "Making children is easy, son. It's raising them that is the hard part."

Although we made time alone a priority, even after the kids came, both Hans and I would say for certain that the years when we had babies and young toddlers were the toughest on our marriage. Our commitment to our marriage was the same. But our closeness was not.

Here is a time of danger in a marriage. A woman's natural need for affection and closeness can in some measure be met in her children. A woman can easily use the precious gift of babies—nursing, rocking, and holding them to try to meet that need for affection. It is normal to love and nurture your baby, but God intends for our *marriage* to be the place where this need for affection as women is met. It is not healthy for parents to seek to have those needs met through their children. Unhealthy attachments and abnormal expectations of children will result.

In view of these challenges, a few special tips for wives and husbands would be good to take note of here:

Special Tip for Women: If you are allowing the intimacy you have with your children to take first place in your emotions, time, and energy, you must take steps to change that. If you are early on in child-rearing, I would challenge you to step back and ask yourself if you are guilty of this. If so, take action. Seek wise counsel from a godly older woman, counselor, or pastor. Then make changes to put your husband first in your heart again. You may need to plan a getaway yourself (without children) and surprise your husband (see suggestions in chapter 10, and don't necessarily leave all the romance to your husband).

If you are further along in your child-rearing years, and this has been your pattern, you have a greater challenge! Your whole family is used to this, and certainly your husband feels like second place (or worse)

RANDY FINALLY TURNED ON HIS RADAR

Randy could tell that Jamie was at the end of her rope. Their two children had been sick on and off all winter, and the middle of the night interruptions were getting to her. Night after night of interrupted sleep can be a living nightmare even in the daytime when the exhaustion gets deeper and deeper.

Finally, one night it got through to Randy that Jamie was on the brink of collapsing. Isn't it amazing what it takes for husbands to finally see that their wives are on the edge—maybe even over the edge and clinging on for dear life. Without her suggesting it, Randy told Jamie that evening as their little Kari was again very ill, that he would stay up with her *all night.* For a guy, this is a real act of love since they don't genetically come by the mothering instinct. What Jamie told us was this: "He really showed me what a great husband and father he is. He not only stayed up with her and held her all night, but he also mothered me so I could truly get a deep night's sleep."

in your life and time. He has probably withdrawn emotionally from you as well, and the strength of your marriage may well be crumbling whether it's evident or not. Although patterns like these are difficult to change, change they must if your marriage is to endure and be all God intends it to be. Ask your husband some straight questions:

(1) How do you feel our relationship has changed since we had children?

(2) Do you feel that I put you first in our home?

(3) Tell me three things I could do to "put you first" in my life?

Special Tips for Men: If you see this as the portrait of your marriage and home, you need to confess where you have failed to get involved in understanding your wife. Recognize her needs for affection, and set aside time for her! Remember how you need to study her as "the feminine one" from 1 Peter 3. This marital closeness is *important* to the Lord, because our oneness reflects to the world, our kids, and even to the angels in some mysterious way, the wonder of Christ's union with His bride, the church! As you learn to actually cherish those feminine ways that make her unique (rather than resisting them), you will benefit in your own outlook as God created her in ways to complement the way He has created you as a man (Gen. 2:18-25). See chapter 10 for more ideas on ways to build closeness in your marriage.

BEING A RESPONDER

I, Donna, see in myself, and the women I have known, a common trait of "responder." In many areas of our lives, women are initiators, including marriage. Anyone who knows me well, knows that I am *no doormat* who waits around to jump and respond to Hans' initiative. So what am I saying? In the area of a woman's needs, and her walking through the days and months of her life, I believe this area is often overlooked, whether purposefully (out of fear of being "politically incorrect") or out of oversight.

Here is what I am saying. I *respond* to Hans. When *he* is on target with God's commands set forth in Scripture (1 Peter 3 and Eph. 5) and is seeking to daily care about me in my world as a woman and wife, I will *respond;* that is, I will *naturally* be more what he needs and wants me to be as a companion, friend, and lover. It is true! When I *know* he is there for me:

❑ **Supporting me**: Backing me up in my authority with the kids.

❑ **Respecting what I do**: In the home—taking care of the food, clothes, kids, cars, and so on—it can be a small gesture.

❑ **Giving me warm affection**: Physical touch, occasional cards, flowers, and so on.

❑ **Relieving my responsibility**: Getting a sitter to get away for an overnight or more, and sometimes taking the initiative to care for the kids *totally* so that I am free to have true "time off."

❑ **Listening to me**: Asking questions and digging to find out where I'm at.

❑ **Sharing with me**: Allowing me to be *close* to him by his communication of *his* world to me.

Then, I truly believe, most men would be *shocked* at the change in their wives! Their wives will *respond* to them in ways they would never have anticipated or even hoped for. Men, do you really want your wife to be there for you in your greatest needs, including sexual intimacy? Then I challenge you to do it! Try out this list on a consistent basis. Your wife will be a happier woman. She will be less crabby and irritable with you and the kids; and you will hear less complaining from her about her work. Although the weight of her responsibilities may not lessen on a regular basis by the changes you make, she will better be able to cope, and will enjoy her varying roles much better.

HERO HUSBANDS WE KNOW

Johnny Miller is the president of Columbia International University in Columbia, South Carolina, and a good personal friend. He and his lovely wife, Jeannie, have one of those special marriages that has stood the test of time and come out strong on the other side of the child-rearing years. He qualifies with flying colors for our hero husband award.

Early in their marriage, with young children in their home, Johnny saw how easily marital intimacy can slip away. He says,

> How true is the television commercial for oil filters, which says, "Pay me now, or pay me later." It's cheaper and easier to maintain an engine than to rebuild it. That's also true of marriage. Intimacy is both the process and product of maintaining a marriage, and it's cheaper than trying to rebuild. Quality time with Jeannie became a premium for me as a young pastor when I discovered I was beginning to get more intellectual and emotional stimulation from both the women and men of the church than from my own wife.
>
> I saw other women only when they were at their best. They listened appreciatively, discussed intelligently. My own wife was too busy with babies to sense my desires, and we were both too stressed out by the growth of the church to have time just for living.
>
> An alarm was going off in my heart. So I arranged a two-day trip alone with Jeannie and confessed what was going on inside. I said that the reason for getting it out into the open was because of my total commitment to her alone. I knew it would hurt her, and it did. It hurt me, too.

We don't enjoy causing pain, but pain is sometimes the can opener to get the good stuff out.

After our tears and talking, we made some commitments to each other that have lasted twenty years. We committed to have at least one 2-hour session weekly when we would be totally alone, look each other in the eye and talk about everything on our hearts. We began to take annual retreats for spiritual and emotional refreshment, and for planning the best use of our time. We had frequent prayer times alone.

We learned to tell the children that they could not butt in when Mom and Dad were talking—something they never did comprehend but which they learned to respect. They also learned to appreciate our dates and our joy in each other. I am sure that gave them a great deal of security as well.

Johnny and Jeannie have a beautiful relationship. Their closeness is obvious. How rare and powerful are his closing words on the intimacy they enjoy: "I still feel as excited about my sweetheart as I did more than 36 years ago when I first winked at her at a friend's wedding. There is no one on earth who knows me better, or to whom I feel closer, or with whom I would rather spend time. The work of developing intimacy with both her and with God have been worth it" (From: "Intimacy and Bucket Seats," *Columbia International University Quarterly*, Winter 1996, pp.1–2).

Powerpoints

One thing we would recommend is getting away from time to time as a couple to debrief on your relationship. Donna and I try to get away for at least one overnight without the children every spring and every fall. Sometimes we are able to manage more than just one night, but at a minimum we need a couple of serious debriefs each year.

What amazes us is how many couples never get away from the children to work on their relationship. We have friends who never use baby-sitters and have never once gone on an overnight alone since the children were born. And then they wonder why nothing is left when the children are grown and gone!

It is not shirking your responsibility before God to have some time away from them occasionally. It is, in fact, one of the best things you can do *for your kids*. When you are alone, here are a few questions that you might want to discuss to get the conversation flowing, with the goal in mind of husbands tuning in to the radar signals of their wives:

PERSONAL RETREAT QUESTIONS

1. On a scale of 1–10 with 1 being weak and 10 being strong, how would you rate our marital relationship? Why did you rate it the way you did?

2. What are some things you would love to do as a woman? What would you like to become that you are not right now? Be specific and let me know some of your hidden dreams.

3. On a scale of 1–10, how would you rate my sensitivity to your needs? Am I a good communicator? How can I improve? Why do you rate me the way you do?

4. What do I do in the home that is a help to you and pleases you? What do I neglect that bothers you the most?

5. If there is one thing you could change about me, what would it be?

6. What are some of the greatest hurts that you carry? What are some of your biggest fears? What about frustrations? Be open with me.

E I G H T
SPECTATORSHIP IN THE HOME
Engaging the Husband's Responsibilities at Home

❑ Husbands have a vested interest in not learning how to do things well around the house. If they do it well, it might become a regular assignment! So men all across the land learn to practice what we call "intentional incompetence."

❑ The libido of the American man is focused almost entirely upon his business so that as a husband he is glad to have no responsibilities.

❑ A strong part of a woman's identity is expressed through her home.

❑ *If I could change one thing about my husband:* "I would change his quiet spectatorship to active participation and inquisitiveness of what's happening in my life and the children's."

Bill Cosby has a classic video of a stage act that is certainly over twenty years old. It is called, "Bill Cosby, Himself," and is one of the staples of the Finzel family's humor collection. After renting it for years, Donna gave me my own copy for my birthday last year. When we really want a laugh, the kind where we have to stop the tape to catch our breath from laughing so hard, we can always count on Bill.

In one of the best routines, called "chocolate cake," Bill's wife wakes him at 6 A.M. one morning to fix the kids' breakfast (they have five kids). Of course, Bill has no interest whatsoever in getting up at that inhumane hour. He grunts and rolls over, going back to sleep. "It is her job. Let her do it," he reasons. In the next moment she is standing over him with a bucket of ice-cold water. "If you don't get up in five seconds and get downstairs and fix them breakfast, I will soak you with this bucket of water!" she screams. All *she* wants is one morning in bed! Is that too much to ask of a father, who leaves you to get the kids out every morning?

Bill finally rolls out of bed with one eye open and goes downstairs in his robe, angrily groping around the kitchen for something to give the kids for breakfast. The first child down, his little eight-year-old daughter, spies the chocolate cake on the counter and says, "Dad, can I have chocolate cake for breakfast?" Of *all the things* in the kitchen, she spotted the cake first even though it was behind him on the counter! "She's got x-ray vision!" Bill begins to think, "Well, actually what is in chocolate cake? Milk. Eggs. Butter. Flour. Sure, why not? Those are, after all, the ingredients of a balanced breakfast." Pretty soon all the children are in the kitchen, and Dad is serving up chocolate cake for everyone for breakfast. As he serves, the children sing in blissful harmony, "*Dad is great—he gave us the chocolate cake! Dad is great—he gave us the chocolate cake!*"

> ## AGREE OR DISAGREE?
>
> *One way to look at it*
>
> "The libido of the American man is focused almost entirely upon his business so that as a husband he is glad to have no responsibilities. . . . It is what I call the laziness of the American man."
>
> —Carl Jung, as quoted in *Woman*, by Charles Swindoll

Things are going great until . . . you guessed it. Mom comes downstairs. Everything falls silent—the party is over. She spots the kids and the chocolate cake. Of course, they turn on Dad, "He made us eat it, Mom!" With fire in her eyes she tells him to *go back to bed*—she will have to feed the kids breakfast herself if she wants it done right. And instead of a problem, Bill scores a success. *Back to bed*—that is what he wanted all along! He can hardly keep the smile on the inside as he charges back up the stairs to their bedroom.

Husbands have a vested interest in not learning how to do things well around the house. If they do it well, it might become a regular assignment! So men all across the land learn to practice what we call "intentional incompetence."

Comedienne Diane Ford put it best: A woman works her tail off all the time. The guy does two things around the house, and he's got to show her, "Honey, look! I fixed the screen! And look over there: I washed my dish! I put my shirt up!" What can the wife say? "Well, why don't we put a little star on the refrigerator?"

One complaint we hear over and over again is wives having to wait on their husbands to fix things around the house. The husband says he will do it (read *promises*), but then neglects to ever get to it. If the wife takes the matter into her own hands, she gets chewed out for (a) not letting him do it, or (b) spending "our good money" to have someone else do it.

Listen to this exchange of one couple:

> **Her:** (at the bedside table stacked high with books yet to be read): Honey, I think I'm going to go out today and get a bookcase for all this stuff. Want to come?

> **Him:** Come? No . . . gee . . . I've got too much to do today. Besides, why spend the money when I can make one myself? How about if I take next Saturday and get some wood and build one. Can it wait until then?

> **Her:** Well, sure. . . .

> [Cut to next Saturday, A.M.]

> **Her:** So, you're gonna make that bookcase today?

> **Him:** Don't bug me. I said I'd get to it . . . soon.

Months go by. No bookcase gets built. Finally in frustration she goes out and buys the bookcase. You know what his response will be:

He gets *really* mad: "What'd you do that for?" he asks. "I told you I'd take care of it."

One wife was so fed up with her husband not picking up after himself that she tried a new approach. Nagging never worked and only annoyed him. "On our anniversary, I gave Chris a card that listed all the wonderful things he was to me—what a great cook he was, how much I admired his patience with the kids, and that I thought he still had the most beautiful blue eyes. At the bottom in really small print, I wrote: "If you could only learn to pick up after yourself, you'd be perfect."

"He laughed when he read it and said, 'I didn't realize. . . . Does my sloppiness really upset you that much?' Can you believe it? Where had he been for the last ten arguments? But he got better after that. And now when he leaves his junk around, I only have to point to it and he gets the message" (*From Good Housekeeping,* March 1996, "Your Husband's Bad Habits," by Sara Nelson, pp. 80–81.)

HER HOME IS HER IDENTITY

A strong part of a woman's identity is expressed through her home. Whether she is consciously aware of it or not, I believe it is true. Her home says to the world, "This is who I am, and here is what I'm like." Considering some *women* are unaware of how strongly their identity is tied to their home, it should not be surprising that *men* are completely baffled by this fact. They say the common, "Oh, you care too much what people think," when they see their wives' seemingly excessive effort to care for her home. Hans will ask if we can have someone over for dinner at the drop of a hat and then get upset when I go into the "get the house ready" mode. He'll say something like, "What's wrong with them seeing how we live in the natural?" Men!

To be fair, some of us truly do get obsessive about our homes "when company is coming." We need to step back and remember our priority of people (including our husbands and kids) above tasks. But men need to look a bit deeper when they feel their wives demand too much when it comes to the home and what they want out of their husbands.

Some women are, of course, more messy by nature. Their personality is more laid back, and they don't even see the mess. Many of these women are super mothers, who are great with crafts and doing other creative activities with their kids. Being like that is, of course, a valid expression of who they are. "Life is messy" as the saying goes. Life is also short, and spending time with our husbands and kids should take priority over a perfect home.

Pity the poor family who lives the other extreme—what I call a "maniac perfectionist" who drives herself and everyone around her crazy with her demands for cleanliness. We all well know that there is absolutely no end to the work of homemaking. Thus a balance must be found to have a truly happy home for all. Remember, women, Scripture commands us to be "given to hospitality." Our home must be not only an "expression of me," but also a place to open willingly and often to others. Even when it's not "finished" in our minds, or as clean as we'd necessarily like, we must make it an open place to share the love of Christ with others. Real life happens here. Our kids' friends, neighbors, the hurting—they all should be coming through our doors.

The easygoing way of messy women may also be a thorn in their husband's side. The Bible warns against laziness and the results of being a sluggard; some women do struggle with this. If you struggle with this, ask the Lord to help you with His fruit of self-control. Then seek out advice and good books on organization and discipline.

Finally, there are also those who struggle with depression, with physical limitations, or the overwhelming demands of many young children. Those women may be unable to keep their home as they would like. They need even more the attention of their husbands in carrying a greater weight in household work.

Hans and I have lived in many homes in our twenty years of marriage. We started out in a "garage apartment" behind the home of a wealthy family in Dallas. In exchange for free rent and utilities, we were "on call" to baby-sit for their two boys on the weekends and occasionally when they went away as a couple. It was certainly our most simple home—two rooms, one of which we shared during the day with the maid, who did the family laundry in it. Since that time, we have lived in eight other homes! It has always been a challenge for us to make each one our own. We are blessed with the same taste and agree on almost every detail. (Yes, we know what a blessing this is. It's nice to actually be alike in some way!) Hans is unusual in how quickly he fixes things and gets to tasks I ask him to do…my "Honey Do Lists." I am very grateful for this.

> ## Top Ten Tip
> *A Cry from One Young Mother*
>
> If I could change one thing about my husband: "I would change his quiet spectatorship to active participation and inquisitiveness of what's happening in my life and the children's."

This chapter probably wouldn't have even made our "Top Ten" except for how strongly this issue came through to us from those wives who completed our survey. These women are very frustrated and feel stuck between a "rock and a hard place" on this issue of husbands helping out and doing their part at home.

Listen to this cry from a young mother on the East Coast. In response to our question, *"If you could change anything about your husband, what would it be?"* she actually made a list for her husband:

1. Change "I love you" statements to actions of love: Help with the dishes, pray with the kids at night, and work with the children to

make them do their chores and have quiet times each day.

2. Change your laziness and TV watching to help with the homework and reading books to the children in the evenings.

3. Change your view that our two separate roles in life don't meet anywhere. You come home each evening with this attitude—"I work all day, and I'm tired at night, and I'm going to relax."

4. Change quiet spectatorship to active participation and inquisitiveness of what's happening in my life and the children's.

Our heart goes out to this friend. She doesn't have the courage to give him this list, and that might not be the right approach anyway. On top of these attitudes that she has to live with, she *home schools their three children*, and a fourth child is on the way! What options does this wife have? Really, with little support from her husband, only two that seem obvious. The two common options seem to be:

Option one: End up being a "nag" because jobs don't get taken care of.

Option two: Forget about it and try to ignore those things that are left undone.

Obviously neither option is good. Proverbs warns over and over again of the damage nagging can do to the family. We believe that nagging creates quarrels nine times out of ten, as seen clearly in these verses. Here are a few powerful admonitions from the Book of Proverbs:

❏   "A quarrelsome wife is like a constant dripping"—Proverbs 19:13.

❏   "Better to live on a corner of the roof than share a house with a quarrelsome wife"—Proverbs 21:9.

❏   "Better to live in a desert than with a quarrelsome and ill-tempered wife"—Proverbs 21:19.

Women, we must be careful not to allow nagging to be a character-istic of our lives. But husbands can also be reminded that "wealth" and "plenty," such as being a workaholic to get ahead financially, don't bring peace into your home either. You need to "engage" yourself; to "carry your share" to enjoy a joyful home with a happy family.

❑   "Better a dry crust with peace and quiet than a house full of feasting,
      with strife"—Proverbs 17:1.

"Forgetting about it" doesn't work either. Sure some women adjust and decide not to let their frustration control them. But neglect on the part of the husband of those household involvements and problems is actually neglect of her. Men, as I already said, realize that your home reflects your wife. She usually cares more than you do that those things get done. Loving her is meeting her needs. Although she may be able to "forget it" for a time, it's possible she may only be stuffing it. Remember all that we said in chapter 7 about how the disappointments or issues in one area of a woman's life often carry over to negatively affect her attitude toward her husband overall. Two of a woman's needs—"financial support" and "family commitment"—fall into this area of carrying your share at home. If you are committed to your wife and family, then you need to willingly support them.

There are two other options for this couple. One is for the wife to pray for her husband that he will change. Ask God to bring some men into his life who can help him see the light. Pray that he will get involved in your church with a men's group that can help. Encourage him to go to Promise Keepers (more on that in a moment). You can also press for the two of you to get some professional counseling. The couple in our story here are headed for trouble, and one of the best things they can do at this stage in their life together is to talk to their pastor or a counselor about their problems.

MONEY CAN'T BUY YOU LOVE

Many men get hung up on the notion that money is the solution to all the family's problems. If they just work harder to bring home more money, then she will be more happy. I am certain that for most of the women I know they would rather have more of their husband's personal attention and involvement at home than more money in the checking account.

The marriage vows we repeated years ago said, "In sickness and in health, for richer or poorer..." We have been in many levels of financial security in our years of marriage. As newlyweds, we struggled to make ends meet even with our super "free-living" situation. Next, we had some years with two incomes in California when we had lots of freedom financially. Then we spent ten years living overseas in Austria on a limited income prescribed by our mission. It was a real challenge to find affordable housing in Vienna during those years. Our housing allowance was limited, and the cost of housing was sky-high in Vienna. We made it a matter of prayer to even be able to find an apartment or house.

The Lord provided each time, and it makes me smile to think how we managed and made each one the three places we lived in Austria into our own Finzel haven. Overall it was fun. Hans and I both have a strong creative side, and we certainly had to use creativity in many of those homes. Our last house in Europe actually had two kitchens, one on each floor. That may sound elegant and convenient, but it was really a major waste of limited space. The house also had an annoying fireplace coming up through the middle of one of the rooms. Solution? Ask the landlord if we could "take out" the kitchen and store it. He said, "Yes, of course!" So we made that cozy former kitchen alcove room above the garage into the nursery for our eighteen-month-old twins. The other problem, the fireplace, actually acted like a great "room divider"! We made half of the room a family and TV room and the other half a playroom for our four kids.

Our point here is that no matter what your financial resources are (or are not), you can make a house a home. You *can* give your wife that place of joy to express herself. Moving ten times in our first twenty years of marriage certainly was not our plan, and is not ideal, but in spite of all that stress and work, we had fun! Much of the joy I feel as I look back on all of those places we lived (in spite of all the moves) comes from our working together to make each one into our Finzel home.

It means so much to me that Hans cares enough about me to help "make it happen," whether that means spending money, wallpapering, putting in extra outlets in a kitchen, or even heavier jobs. I'm very blessed that one of the most natural ways Hans expresses his love for me is in this way.

PROMISE KEEPERS TO THE RESCUE

For several years now, Promise Keepers' meetings have been having a powerful impact upon tens of thousands of men and on their families. In our church, the first summer only five or six men went, but our pastor allowed them to share the impact of the conference with our church body on a Sunday night soon after their return. Wow! We were amazed at the changes and new commitments to the Lord and to their marriages these men had made. It had truly been a taste of revival for them.

The next summer, well over 100 men from our church attended, and the impact upon them and our church was multiplied! As a woman, I find it most ironic that much of what has been portrayed in the news media regarding Promise Keepers has been jaded and downright untrue. Contrary to their cries of "male chauvinism" and "power feeding" for men, the outcome has in my view been one of the best things that has ever happened to *help women!* Why? Because the speakers have challenged these men to be who God intends them to be! Men of God, who seek to know Him, be accountable to other men for keeping their lives pure, and honoring their commitments to be better husbands and fathers.

We personally know men who went "kicking and screaming"— "forced" to go by their wives or family members to Promise Keepers. These men were skeptics, who I believe were also fearful of what it would mean to go to such a conference with 40,000 to 60,000 men. Yet, in every case, they were revolutionized in a positive way! Several of them came to faith in Christ. Others opened their hearts to their brothers for the first time with their own struggles as they shared meals and driving time together. So, as a wife and woman, I for one am thrilled to be counted among the thousands of women who want our husbands and sons there every chance they can! Ladies, encourage your husbands to go and do everything you can to make it happen. The message is loud and clear at Promise Keepers: Men are to be involved as husbands and fathers in the home in substantial ways.

HERO HUSBANDS WE KNOW

Donna and I have the rare and valuable privilege of both being from families where the mother and dad stayed together their whole married lives in a positive and nurturing marriage. In chapter 4 you heard about Donna's dad and his spiritual leadership in the home. He and Mom Bubeck have been married almost fifty years, and their relationship is truly a tribute to doing it right.

I, Hans, grew up in a very different home than Donna did, being a first-generation American living in the home of immigrants from Germany. My parents moved to America right after World War II to work for the U.S. government in building missiles in the budding space program. My father's boss was Dr. Werner Von Braun, and he and a group of scientists and engineers were brought to America after

World War II to begin the U.S. space program. My family, along with 100 other German families, immigrated to and settled in Huntsville, Alabama, on the southern rim of the beautiful Smoky Mountains.

Our home was a traditional German home, where we spoke the language of our parents. My experience was typical of a third-culture kid, in many ways similar to the lives of missionary children growing up in foreign cultures. It was a good childhood, and to this day I believe I model my own role as husband and father based upon the example of my dad even more than I realize it.

My dad, whom we called "Vati"—German for "daddy"—was certainly not a perfect man. The older I get the more I realize that some of my own inadequacies are the same inadequacies that I saw in him. The awesome power of genetics! One thing my dad was great in was being involved in the home as a helping father and husband to my mom. My dad had an intense career in the U.S. space program. You can imagine the pressure during the years when they were building rockets to put us on the moon. I remember hearing the roaring blast of rocket engines being tested at the NASA space center in Huntsville, even though the test stands were twenty miles from our home!

After the Apollo program came the space shuttle, and there was always plenty to do with long intense hours of work. And yet I could always tell that my father loved his family more than he loved his work. I also noticed through the years how much he loved being alone with my mom as they would take trips together to different places around the world. They loved traveling together more than any other recreational experience.

When my father was home, he was really home. He didn't have hobbies or lots of personal friends who took him away from home when he wasn't working. He was busily engaged in the evenings and every weekend in taking care of the house and making it a home. I remember his Saturday morning trips to the hardware store to gather the necessary equipment for that weekend's "honey do" list. He took good care of everything that broke down in the home, and he did it quickly and proficiently. I can also remember the countless hours he spent working with me on my go-carts and then later numerous collections of motorcycles, which I acquired as a teenager. He was there for me, and he was engaged in my life when I needed him.

Unfortunately, my father was a smoker, and he died of lung cancer in 1984. My mother never remarried because as far as she was concerned, there could never be a man who would even closely measure up to the stature of my father. To this day she worships him and, of course, misses him intensely. Vati taught me a lot of great values. He showed me how to be a good husband and father who engages in the things that need to be done around the house to keep the family corporation operational. He wasn't perfect, and I'm not perfect. But I do thank him for providing such a strong example in this important area of husbandhood.

Powerpoints

This chapter is one that could easily be seen as a put-down on men. Women hate to nag their husbands, but the alternatives are none the more appealing. Husbands' working in the home is an area that many men don't want to hear about, but it's an issue that is very real and on the front burner for most wives.

What's a husband and father to do? In two words, "Focused engagement." We like the way our friend on the East Coast puts it: *Change quiet spectatorship to active participation and inquisitiveness of what's happening in my life and the children's.* A few other tips to help you along your way:

❑ **Remember her view of your home**—everything about your home matters to your wife because it reflects her! Part of respecting and loving her is to understand how important this is to her.

❑ **Don't procrastinate**—whatever that means in your life, whether you set a three-day limit to do what she asks for fix-it jobs or "do it now" in the case of taking the garbage out or other small requests.

❑ **Take the initiative**—surprise her by doing tasks without being asked. As we said earlier, she is not the maid. Doing dishes, picking up (or telling kids to pick up) things, cleaning bathrooms, and so on are not exclusively *her* job description.

❑ **Do some research by asking her**—What needs to be done that I could do tonight? What are the few things that bother you the most that, if I did, would mean the most to you?

❑ **Set aside one Saturday a month for projects**—Many dads spend Saturdays with kids at the ball games. Why not make one Saturday a month a day for those projects she needs done around the house?

❑ **If you're not going to do it soon**—Let her hire someone else to do it. As in the case of the wife with the bookshelf or the woman who wanted to pay to have someone clean the windows, if you're just going to make promises that you can't keep, then free her up to spend the money. She is happy, you're off the hook, and life is good.

❑ **Go to Promise Keepers**—Men, sign up and go with your friends. Women, do whatever you can to make it possible for your husband to get there.

NINE

I Wear the Pants in This Family

The Marriage Partnership—
Shared Leadership in the Home

❏ Marriage is a partnership, not a dictatorship.

❏ Today we find many people talking about the
shifting paradigms of decision-making in the
home. Much of it has to do with women's roles in
the work force.

❏ The biblical picture of submission, as it relates to
marriage, is always coupled with our submission
to our Lord Jesus Christ.

❏ Submission is not where the wife willingly
becomes a rug her husband can wipe his feet on.
Neither is it where the husband is barking orders
and the wife jumps in fear at the sound of his
voice.

T he world out there has a lot of skewed views of man in the home. For example: "I'm loud, and I'm vulgar, and I wear the pants in this house because somebody's got to...." a line from Edward Albee's play, *Who's Afraid of Virginia Woolf?* Or how about this one, a proverb from the Old Deep South, "Wives should be kept barefoot in the summer and pregnant in the winter."

For starters, Donna and I both wear pants around the house most of the time. On any given day you'll find us in our jeans—hers will be Gap and mine will be Levi's 560's, but we are definitely both into pants.

In a recent report in *Good Housekeeping* magazine, we discovered that many people are talking about the shifting paradigms of decision-making in the home today. Much of it has to do with women's roles in the work force. According to a ground-breaking study released last year by the Families and Work Institute, women earn half or more of the income in an astonishing 44 percent of dual-earner homes. And the most recent figures from the U.S. Bureau of Labor Statistics for 1993 show that 22 percent of women make more than their husbands—up from 17 percent in 1987. The magazine article goes on to conclude:

> The numbers reveal a sea of change in American society that is turning
> the traditional family upside down. And more than money is at issue.
> When wives are the main providers, couples are forced to rethink the
> way they make decisions and take care of their children. For most cou-
> ples, that means power shifts, negotiation, and sacrifice. Some hus-
> bands—and wives—feel humiliated or disappointed because they are
> not living the lives they expected to. Others feel emancipated by the
> changes, preferring to share the rewards and responsibilities of support-
> ing a family, to being locked into old stereotypes (*Good Housekeeping*,
> January 1996, p. 93).

Hans and I operate our lives as a team. Because I am home full time,
our lives could be viewed as the vanishing traditional American family,
where dad works and mom is at home with the children. But as "Baby
Boomers," we have also adopted many of the good changes in the new
roles of our generation. Hans has always been very active with the
kids from birth! He has willingly been part of doing diapers, dishes,
and other domestic duties. At the same time, although Hans manages
the finances in our household, he makes sure that I am well aware of
any important financial matters. I arrange for the upkeep of our family
van and have done the research and purchasing of some of the major
household items. We split up the work and have learned to trust each
other and read each other through the years.

The two most important passages of Scripture that form the foundation of our view of our marriage have to do with this issue of mutual
value and submission to one another:

❏ **On the issue of equal worth**—Genesis 1:27: "So God created man in
   His own image, in the image of God He created him; **male and female
   He created them.**"—This verse from the first chapter of the Bible lays
   the groundwork for our mutual respect for each other. We are equally

created in the image of God and therefore match in all matters of worth and humanity. When it comes to worth, we know that although there is an authority structure in our home, it in no way lessens the value and contribution of each member of the family.

❑ **On the issue of mutual submission**—Ephesians 5:21-25: "**Submit to one another** out of reverence for Christ. **Wives**, submit to your husbands as to the Lord. For the husband is the head of the wife as Christ is the head of the church, his body, of which He is the Savior. Now as the church submits to Christ, so also wives should submit to their husbands in everything. **Husbands**, love your wives, just as Christ loved the church and gave Himself up for her."—In this passage revisited once again, we point out that it begins with *mutual submission*. Following the admonition to "be filled with the Spirit" earlier in Ephesians 5:18, Paul showed that a couple walking in the Spirit will lovingly submit with care and concern for the needs of their spouse.

So how do these principles make our marriage a team? To summarize these two bottom-line operating principles of our marriage, we believe that:

❑ 1. We are both of equal value and worth before God and have equal weight in our marriage.

❑ 2. Though we view Hans as the head of our home, we submit to one another's needs as we walk in the Spirit out of reverence for Christ.

Defining Mutual Submission

Submission is a topic that has been covered very well in many Christian books today. Although the subject is a hot topic, our purpose here is not to go into the depths of that discussion. We do, however, want to be sure to convey our view of what submission is not.

Simply put, it is not where the wife willingly becomes a rug her husband can wipe his feet on. Neither is it where the husband is barking orders and the wife jumps in fear at the sound of his voice.

As it relates to marriage, the biblical picture of submission is always coupled with our submission to our Lord Jesus Christ. We all need authority in our lives. This is God's plan. Since we are believers, Jesus Christ is the Lord of our lives. We willingly and joyfully submit to Him because we trust Him, we love Him, we know He has our best interests at heart. The submission that a wife is to have to her husband is to be like that. This kind of submission is similar to what I described in chapter 7 regarding the way in which I respond to Hans. As Hans follows the Lord and obeys God in caring for my needs and in seeking to lovingly lead our family in spiritual growth, I willingly come alongside him in agreement. Indeed, he values my input.

> ## THE PORTRAYAL OF A WOMAN IN THE BIBLE
> *by Charles Swindoll*
>
> After reading all through the Scriptures while looking at a woman's role, he concluded:
>
> "Except in a few isolated and special occasions, the women who appear in the Scripture are competent, secure, qualified people who had responsible roles to fill and in doing so played a vital part in shaping of history and in the development of lives. They are beautiful examples of humanity at every economic level of society."
>
> From *Woman: A Person of Worth & Dignity,* by Charles Swindoll, p. 9.

Rarely has it been necessary in our marriage for Hans to "assert" his authority or tell me I need to go his way on an issue. In twenty years such a need might have occurred only a handful of times. Nevertheless, I view him as the one whom God holds ultimately responsible for us as a couple and family. Therefore, I respect his final authority.

We work through situations mutually respecting the input and point of view of the other. As a matter of fact, Hans has often come to realize my more "feminine" point of view and "intuition" as one of his greatest assets. Because my very strengths and people skills are his weakest points, he deeply values and seeks out my insights on most situations. In that way, as Hans said, we both "wear the pants" in our family. But there is also a certain comfort I have in knowing "the buck stops with Hans." If I've had it with the kids, he'll deal with them. If a decision we've made financially doesn't work out, he usually has to bear the weight of it. Is that weakness on my part? Am I contributing to male chauvinism in purporting this view? I strongly believe the answer is *no*. Just as we experience a great security and strength as believers because of our trust in the Lord and His love for us, wives can know the same joy in this kind of submissive, giving relationship with her husband.

I don't think I always submit in the way I've just described. Nor has Hans always necessarily carried his part as he should. I'm certain most of you identify with us and can think of times you have either been rebellious to God's ways or you have taken the easy way out by shrugging off responsibility. Nevertheless, we need to remember the impact our success or failure in this area has on our kids. They learn by our example for better or worse. They will model their own marriages after ours. If the husband is "lording it" over his wife either by quietly refusing to listen to her point of view or openly confronting her "rebellion" with his "superior" viewpoint, he is wrong. If the wife berates her husband in front of others (especially the children), or if she quietly goes her own way refusing to consider her husband's desires but doing her own thing, she is wrong. They will both reap what they sow.

Paul put it best: "Wives, submit to your husbands, as is fitting in the Lord. Husbands, love your wives and do not be harsh with them" (Col. 3:18-19). Then he continued, "Since you know that you will receive an inheritance from the Lord as a reward. It is the Lord Christ you are serving" (v. 24). If we sow to ourselves, in disobedience to God's Word, we will reap what is described in verse 25: "Anyone who does wrong will be repaid for his wrong, and there is no favoritism." I like to think of "favoritism" as related to "excuses." We won't have any excuses when we refuse to walk this way!

DECISION-MAKING

Perhaps the best way for us to explain how we practice this type of "mutual respect decision-making" is to tell the story of a major life decision we had to make five years ago. It was one of the biggest career/life moves we have ever made. Looking back at it now, we realize that how we made the decision is almost as important to us as the decision we actually made. We were both equal stakeholders in the process, and when it was finally a done deal, we both had and continue to have a great peace in that decision as the right one.

Decision-making for us has had a different face each time we've made a big one. I believe we've grown in this area through the years of our marriage. One of the most difficult and important decisions of our life came to us as the Lord was obviously closing the chapter of our work in Eastern Europe. For some reason, just as we were realizing that it was clearly time to move on to a new job and a new challenge, we received at least five strong feelers for new opportunities. Although we'd not indicated we were ready to move on, these organizations sought us out just at that time. They were all viable options with exciting possibilities for both Hans and me.

Our usual practice of talking through the details and praying through the options was a part of this decision-making process. But one difference was that we needed to keep many of the details of the opportunities completely confidential. This made seeking wise counsel very limited. Furthermore, Hans' commitment was whatever choice we made would be the very best one for me, especially, and for the children as well. So he made sure we consulted together on all the angles of each option, and he made very clear to me that in this particular decision he would not consider anything unless it would offer me the greatest potential to use my gifts. As he expressed it to me, his basic attitude was: "This is a decision we both have to make in our heart of hearts. I will not talk you into anything."

As we shared together, Hans came to describe each option as different "rafts" floating on the lake of our life. One by one, each raft except for two became burdened down with weights (various negative reasons) and sunk out of the running over a period of about three months. We were then left with two floating rafts. Each was highly desirable. One of the organizations flew Hans back to the U.S. for an in-depth interview. He was also able to visit the other one, and he came back to Vienna very sure deep inside which one was right for us. But I had no idea he knew! At that point, just between him and the Lord Hans decided he would not tell me but would trust the Lord to place in my heart the right one as well. I was actually leaning toward the one he was *not* inclined to take, but was still open to both.

As the process was heating up for a deadline, we set aside two days to seek the Lord with prayer and fasting, promising not to speak of the decision again until we'd completed those two set-aside days. Finally, we drove to a Vienna park to share our hearts once again. Just in those two days, the Lord brought together in me some reading and Scripture to clearly confirm His leading to me. As we sat together in our van (the only "private place") in the pouring rain, Hans asked me which option I believed was the one the Lord had for us. I told him my conclusion. It was the same as his, as I soon found out. He told me then and only then that he had been convinced of it for several weeks. But his attitude was that only if God showed me directly would we walk through the door together.

I can't express clearly enough how powerful it was to me that Hans *honored* my needs and *respected* my insights! He also demonstrated faith in the Lord to entrust me to Him and showed honor for my own walk with the Lord by leaving things in His hands. He refused to manipulate me or place his own position and calling above the plans the Lord would have for me in our next place of ministry.

THEY'RE NOT ALL HEROES

We have tried to focus each chapter on a "Hero Husband" to lend a positive slant to a book that might appear to be "husband bashing." We will do the same later in this chapter. First, however, we also want to share a true story of a couple we have known who have had a tragic marriage that did not turn out well. Many details have been altered to protect their privacy. Though worse than some, this story personifies the destruction to a marriage and home when a husband and wife do not live according to the plan the Lord has provided as we just described—not with submission, respect, yielded love, and consideration, but with selfishness, rebellion, harshness, and bitterness. It reminds us of Proverbs 17:22: "A cheerful heart is good medicine, but a crushed spirit dries up the bones."

Mandy and Brent were married for twelve years. They have two children, an eleven-year-old son, and a nine-year-old daughter. They met in their church singles group. They grew close as they worked together in music, enjoying the gifts of each other, and admiring what they saw in each other. They soon began a dating relationship. Things were a bit rocky from the start for them, but they wrote it off to their mutually strong personalities. Before long Brent proposed and Mandy accepted. Even so, doubts plagued Mandy. Her parents' marriage had ended in divorce. Brent was just happy to have the exclusive love of Mandy; she was quite a "catch" for him. Their singles leader and other friends warned them to wait awhile before getting married. Putting all

advice and doubts aside, however, Brent and Mandy married the following summer.

Within the first year, both Brent and Mandy knew they had made a
big mistake. The very concerns that had aroused doubt in Mandy
were now her life. Brent, whose brother and father had died when he
was a baby, was the only child of a widowed mother. He soon resent-
ed any outside interests and friends Mandy had, feeling jealous of her
time and love. Their previous goal of working in music together had
quickly evaporated. Brent had decided not to pursue further education
and refused to see Mandy pursue her professional goals. Giving up on
his own previous goals, he decided instead to try his hand at selling
automobiles. As a moody and mostly self-absorbed man, he was not
able to make a living at sales.

Their two children had arrived much too quickly for both of them.
Mandy tried to help make ends meet by waitressing a few times a
week, but the resentment between them was thick. Brent complained
that Mandy didn't "support" him and would not "submit" to his leadership. Mandy struggled with Brent's expectations that she treat him as
the "king" of her world. He withheld love as punishment for her lack
of submission and service toward him. Brent left most of the child
care and training to Mandy, only relating to the kids as a "doting
daddy," with pet names that suited babies and toddlers, but which
quickly grew old as the kids grew older.

The years went by. Both Mandy and Brent grudgingly accepted
their lot together since, as "committed Christians," divorce was not an
option for either of them. But their marriage had become a cold war.
The bitterness each felt for the other in their own minds, they attrib-
uted to the other's failure to *obey Scripture*. Brent convinced himself that
their whole problem from day one had been Mandy's refusal to "submit" to him. To him, she was living in sin since she had rebelled
against his "leadership." Mandy, on the other hand, was sure Brent was

incapable of ever loving her as "Christ loved the church." He was too busy loving himself and correcting her and the kids to actually love them. His harshness and sharp comments cut Mandy deeply.

In their eleventh year of marriage, Mandy fell seriously ill. Mandy knew she needed emotional and spiritual healing as well as physical healing. She and Brent agreed to go for marriage counseling. They found a wonderful counselor with whom they could both be open. But the bitter years and pain have definitely done their damage.

None of us know how much the pain of a "crushed spirit" contributed to Mandy's illness, but Scripture clearly does correlate emotional and spiritual health with physical health. We cannot expect to live with anger, pain, resentment, and hurt forever without eventual consequences. This painful story should put up warning signals to all of us. We hope it will give you pause to "stop, look, listen, and seek."

❑ **Stop**—Are you struggling with each other in the area of submission?

❑ **Look**—Review Ephesians 5 to check your marriage against the truth of God's Word. Are you willing to give and love your spouse and not demand your own way? Have you allowed distance and coldness to grow?

❑ **Listen**—Ask your spouse: How do you view our roles in our marriage and home? Men, ask: Am I too demanding or harsh with you? Do you feel that I "lord it over you" in our marriage? What changes would help you most? Women, ask: Do you sense my respect for you? What could I do to honor you as my husband? What changes would help you most?

❑ **Seek**— Professional help from a biblical counselor if your marriage is on the rocks.

Remember Ephesians 4:26-27: " 'In your anger do not sin': Do not let the sun go down while you are still angry, and do not give the devil a foothold." Dr. Paul Meier, respected psychiatrist, author, and godly husband, makes a powerful statement about these verses. In the many years of his practice as a doctor of body and mind, he has found that many diseases, including cancer, are "caused by not obeying this clear command of Scripture." Anger is meant to be dealt with. If it is not, it will eventually weaken the immune system and illness will result!

Furthermore, if we allow anger to rule us, we will be in danger of actually giving Satan grounds against us through our unforgiving spirit. He will seek to use that anger to further damage us and our relationships.

HERO HUSBANDS WE KNOW

Now on to a more encouraging story. Same potential for destruction, but with a much brighter outcome. David and Jenny are both highly talented individuals. In their early years of marriage both had impressive jobs in corporate America. They each had their place to flourish; they enjoyed their life together immensely. David, strongly driven in his job, was also disciplined in managing their good income to invest it for their future.

Several years later they decided to start their family. When their daughter arrived, they agreed they wanted Jenny to stay at home to raise her. Within weeks of the arrival of their baby, David and Jenny made a major move for David's career. The adjustment of new motherhood was compounded for Jenny by the shock of a totally new environment, after leaving her career position as well. She had a tough time. David's success and responsibilities went on, but he was taken by surprise at the struggle Jenny was facing. His high-powered, successful wife was showing new sensitivities and needs. Yet he plowed ahead full bore, placing some expectations upon Jenny that she could not meet. Although David believed, in theory, in loving Jenny, respecting her in her new role, and sharing all decision-making with her, Jenny did not feel those things from him. They had some painful times and misunderstandings, and sometimes the state of their marriage discouraged them deeply.

So what changed the situation? Commitment! The commitment that David and Jenny had to their marriage and to the Lord. That commitment was what pushed them to find answers to the misunderstandings and to make needed changes during a difficult time in their marriage. David arranged to go with his friend to Promise Keepers. Even after the birth of their son, things continued to improve. David was a great father, and he was growing in understanding of his responsibility to meet the needs of his wife. Their godly pastor recommended "Marriage Encounter," as he had seen the tremendous results the marriage retreat had produced in many marriages. David and Jenny scheduled the weekend, not really knowing what to expect. They returned to tell us that their marriage had been transformed. They even asked us to please recommend "Marriage Encounter" in this book.

We consider David a "hero husband." Unlike so many men who are unwilling to consider their need to change and grow, David sought out excellent resources. David opened his life to these lessons. He has grown markedly in his ability to respond well as he has sought the Lord for His help. He's been a testimony to those who know him in his loving relationship to his wife, Jenny. The Lord continues to move David out of some of his more natural negative patterns with obvious positive results. He and Jenny are a very effective team whose love for the Lord and commitment to growth are sharper than ever because of their great gifts!

Powerpoints

I. For husbands:

Your position of authority in the home is sacred and comes with a great deal of responsibility. Do not use your place for dictatorship but for leadership in your partnership with your wife.

2. For wives:

Consider how you can lovingly submit to your husband in ways that support him. If you find that you live in a difficult marriage situation, pray for grace to do what is right, and pray for him that God will change his wrongful attitudes.

3. For both of you:

Think about some of the issues raised in this chapter and write down your own convictions about them. Here are several questions to ponder:

❏ In our marriage, do we view the husband as being the head of the home?

❏ If so, why? In what ways do we mean that he is the head?

❏ As the head of the home, what is the man's unique responsibility before God to fulfill that role?

❏ In the issue of submission, what does the Bible (as in Eph. 5) mean when it is asks wives to submit to their husbands? What does this mean in real life in your marriage?

Finally, if you sense that there is a real problem in your marriage in this area, work through this three-step list that we shared earlier in this chapter:

❑ **Stop**—Are you struggling with each other in the area of submission?

❑ **Look**—Review Ephesians 5 to check your marriage against the truth of God's Word. Are you willing to give and love your spouse and not demand your own way? Have you allowed distance and coldness to grow?

❑ **Listen**—Ask your spouse: How do you view our roles in our marriage and home? Men, ask: Am I too demanding or harsh with you? Do you feel that I "lord it over you" in our marriage? What changes would help you most? Women, ask: Do you sense my respect for you? What could I do to honor you as my husband? What changes would help you most?

❑ **Seek**—Don't be afraid to ask for help with your marriage. Talk to your pastor. Seek a professional couselor's help. Attend a transforming "Marriage Encounter" weekend.

TEN

MISSING THE CHANCE FOR ROMANCE

The Rewards of Dating and Romance in Your Relationship

❑ All work and no play can make marriages a very dull place to be.

❑ Dating in marriage is the ongoing courtship that re-wins your spouse over and over again.

❑ Two people can have a physical relationship without ever being intimate; and conversely, two people can grow into intimacy without departing into sexuality.

❑ The beautiful children who are God's blessing and the very product of our love, can snuff out the flames of passion that got it all going.

Last night I took Donna out on a date. We went to see the Chicago Bulls at the United Center in downtown Chicago. Just the two of us, without the tribe in tow. Of course, the Bulls won and that helped top off a great evening together.

We have short dates and long dates, sometimes just a cup of coffee, often dinner out for just the two of us. Every once in a while we will farm out the kids and have a whole weekend away from the children. We love them, but face it: Their mom and dad are much better parents if they keep their marriage alive. The best thing we can do for our children is to keep our marriage healthy and happy.

Not long ago our getaway was three days on a beach in Southern California. During those times I sometimes say to Donna, "Oh, yes, *now* I remember, you're that spunky girl I married twenty years ago!" She, more than me, has the chance in those moments to climb out of her "mother" role and back into the courtship and carefree role that sparked the romance to begin with. Dating is one of the best ways we have found to keep our marriage fresh. It gives us time to communicate, and it lets Donna know I want to be with her. We do things together that we used to do before life became so serious and full of family responsibility.

Have you ever tried to calculate how much of your communication with your spouse is about family matters, bills, problems, and broken things that need fixing? These are the surface things that consume life and often account for 99 percent of communication between husband and wife. When was the last time you had tender moments of personal talk about how each other is *doing?* Dating in marriage is the ongoing courtship to re-win your spouse over and over.

Nothing Kills Dating Like Kids Do

Life has its strange ironies. Dating leads to love and love to marriage. Marriage usually brings kids, who can stifle the intimate love that started the whole process to begin with. The dating is over. Done. Finished. The beautiful children, who are God's blessing and the very product of our love, can snuff out the flames that got it all going.

Life changes drastically in a marriage when children arrive. Hans and I had talked about wanting four children when we were newly married. That changed quickly after the birth of our first child, Mark.

In our early years of marriage after graduate school, we were in a ministry in Long Beach, California. Hans was on a church staff and I worked full time for "Oilwell Division of U.S. Steel Corp." Without the responsibility of children, we shared daily and deeply about our work. Hans knew details about my work and relationships at Oilwell; I, in turn, worked side by side with him in ministry.

As we began building a ministry to young married couples, we planned retreats and getaways with our growing group of couples. Our marriage grew, and the Lord gave us the joy of helping young couples grow in maturity in their relationships with Christ and with each other.

The freedom we all had, we took great advantage of, spending time as a group, going out together after church, and enjoying hours of deep fellowship. Only three couples in our group had children. They each had only one child. Their children tagged along, and we all enjoyed them immensely. After one of the couples had another child, we saw their involvement change! Often they wouldn't be able to go out with us. The kids were sick or had to go to bed. We didn't understand very well, but we tried to adjust, although we missed their fellowship.

We observed the change that children made in the lives of our friends, but certainly did not comprehend the true impact until several years later when our own son arrived. As we soon came to realize, *the adjustment of having a child is much greater than the adjustment of getting married and living with another person as a mate.*

After several years of wonderful ministry in Long Beach, we knew

> ### TOP TEN TIP
> *A Surprise Night Out*
>
> From a wife in Arizona:
>
> "One thing that would mean a great deal to me would be if Randy would surprise me every once in a while with a romantic night out. Just whisk me away with a carefully thought-out plan that would show me he cares about the romance in our relationship."

our deep heart's desire to serve overseas behind the Iron Curtain was growing. We applied and were appointed to serve with CBInternational in the summer of 1980 as their first missionaries to Eastern Europe. We said good-bye to our friends, ministry, and my job in the late summer of 1981, and landed in Vienna, Austria, in September, 1981. I was six months pregnant with our first child.

What a shock parenthood was! For six years we had enjoyed our independence and involvement in each other's worlds. Overnight, this precious new life entrusted to our care by the Lord had turned our world upside-down!

ME? SELF-CENTERED?

I, Donna, remember clearly that one of the most amazing realities that hit me was how this little person confronted me with the depth and power of my own self-centeredness. By his very nature as a helpless, 100 percent dependent little baby, Mark's needs forced themselves upon me. *My* own needs and desires, and those of Hans', had to come second. It was just the physical realities of caring for a newborn baby. A very physically exhausting experience. Whew!

The fact that I had never been home full time in our years of marriage magnified the shock of parenthood for me. Many women go through these two major adjustments at the same time: becoming a mother and leaving the work force. It's a double whammy on the self-confidence for sure! Added to those two adjustments was the stress of a new culture, new language, and the reality of being a "foreigner." Then, add to that (as if the potential for depression is not enough already), a typical day of Vienna winter was what we called "the gray gloom," and you had one reeling new mom. I remember telling other friends that now that Hans and I had met the reality of

> ### HOW BAD CAN IT GET?
>
> After thirty years of marriage, the wife was ready to finally throw in the towel. "I have had it living with you," she moaned in disgust. "You never tell me you love me. It has been years since I have heard those three words come out of your mouth."
>
> In a stoic, cool manner the husband replied, "Look, I told you I loved you when we got married—if I change my mind, I'll let you know."

parenthood, we were no longer considering the possibility of having four kids. We said "Maybe, just *maybe*, we'll have two!"

In Vienna, we were part of a team of missionaries from thirteen different missions, all working together in a ministry called "BEE," or Biblical Education by Extension. Our leader was Dr. Jody Dillow. His wife, Linda, was my mentor and friend, and as the mother of three school-age children, Linda's wisdom on motherhood was my salvation on many a rough day in those early days of adjustment to my new life. One area that Linda was committed to, beyond all else, was the need for marriage to have first place in our lives! In spite of the needs and demands of Mark on Hans and I, she emphasized that we *must* put our marriage first.

Linda put her words in action by volunteering to baby-sit Mark for us when he was only about a month old so we could have our first "date." I remember the strange feeling it was to leave Mark and go out with Hans alone. We enjoyed a wonderful couple of hours of just sharing together and focusing on each other. Of course, we also talked about our precious son, but we were alone! This was a good breaking point for us, and from that time on we reestablished dating as a regular part of our married life.

That was fifteen years ago, but the lessons have stuck with us. We're so grateful that at that time in our lives Linda and Jody were there for us with their admonitions. They lived the example of laying aside other responsibilities, especially parenthood, to give focused attention to their mate and marriage. We began a pattern that has proven to be the key to the growth and ongoing closeness of our marriage. We *made* time to be together alone. In fact, we highly recommend Linda's book that has been a great resource for wives for a couple of decades now: *Creative Counterpart* (Thomas Nelson: Nashville, 1977).

DON'T BE AFRAID TO LEAVE THEM ALONE

We think that by now you get the picture that we both believe dating *must* be a priority all through a marriage! We believe this is one of the most common and damaging failures couples make after they have children. They fail to set aside time for each other. It seems impossible to schedule, and it's hard emotionally to "let go" of parenting, even for a few hours or a night away. But couples often allow the daily reality of parenting young children to take precedence over their marriage. If they do that as a lifelong pattern, there will be *no relationship left* when the kids are gone and the empty nest is also empty of any abiding relationship.

Men, do you know how much your wife needs to know you value her? Time alone with her—focused on her and your relationship with her—communicates mountains of love and affection to her. Even if you can't see it, *relationship* is what she needs all your married lives. She won't know it if you don't take action to "take her away" alone.

This issue of *relationship* is what seems to puzzle many men. They don't seem to need it, but the wife can't get enough of it. Perhaps the wisdom of Dave Barry is appropriate here:

Tips for Women: How to Have a Relationship with a Guy

Contrary to what many women believe, it's fairly easy to develop a long-term stable, intimate and mutually fulfilling relationship with a guy. Of course, this guy has to be a Labrador retriever. With human guys, it's extremely difficult. This is because guys don't really grasp what women mean by the term *relationship*.

We're not talking about different wavelengths here. We're talking about different *planets*, in completely different *solar systems*. A woman cannot communicate meaningfully with a man about their relationship any more than she can meaningfully play chess with a duck. Because the sum total of man's thinking on this particular topic is as follows: Huh? (From *Dave Barry's Complete Guide to Guys*, Random House, 1995)

Guys are pretty thickheaded about this thing we call relationship. Our journey into this adventure began twenty years ago. Donna and I were married in 1975. We dated for several months and then had a year-long engagement before our actual wedding. During the year of engagement, I was attending Dallas Seminary in Dallas, Texas, and she was in Columbia, South Carolina. We made the best of the long-distance relationship and tried to snatch some quality time together during school breaks. After our wedding we settled into life together in Dallas while I was finishing my master's degree. Though the studies were tough, I made the decision early on in our marriage that I would always go to bed with Donna when it was time for lights out. In fact, in those early years, I remember how comfy-cozy it was that we could actually go to sleep with our toes touching. A good-night kiss might seem like something simple, but it is a strong statement of the intimacy of a marriage as the years go on.

That little habit became a lifelong commitment: to always go to bed together each night. One wife wrote us about a practice that her husband has that greatly frustrates her in this arena. It started when they were in school together. He seemed to have developed a habit of going to bed late because of studying, which led her to feel that he was taking time away from their relationship. As the years have gone on—decades—since those years of study, the habit never changed and an invisible barrier, what we could probably best describe as lack of intimacy, developed.

Going to bed together at night might seem like a small thing, but if it is a consistent pattern for many years, it can communicate a major lack of relationship. For this one couple, the husband next began to come home late for supper and told his wife to go ahead and have dinner with the family without him. One by one, the fires of romance and togetherness in their relationship went out. Today she cries out in desperation as a very lonely wife and mother.

Dr. Ed Wheat in *Love Life* has this to say about those little touches of affection like holding hands on a date, like putting your arm around your wife at the movies, and things like toes touching in bed late at night:

> Many couples who build an intense love relationship by caressing while dating often quit affectionate touching after marriage. The reason? Now they are using touch only as a sexual signal to communicate readiness to make love. At other times they carefully stay apart lest an affectionate gesture be misinterpreted.

TOP TEN DATE TIP

Try Taking Her Shopping at HER Favorite Store to Show Your Love
. . . We Guys Know What That Means!

I can't shop with women. I just get tired. I walk into the women's wear department of any store and my energy just goes south. I'm suddenly seven and in the backseat of the family station wagon, being lulled to sleep by the hum of the road.

There's something about fluorescent lights in malls that makes me very weak. It's like they're made of kryptonite. (However, fluorescent lights in electronics stores make me feel suddenly energetic.) Women know this. That's why, instead of letting you go off and do your own shopping, they make you sit in those little student punishment seats by the dressing rooms. Then they waltz out in some . . . frou-frou and say, "What do you think?"

You muster the stock answer. "Nice. Very nice." And then you follow with the appropriate shared "nod and smile" to the exhausted husband in the other chair.

From Tim Allen, *Don't Stand Too Close to a Naked Man*, p. 180.

Couples must break the habit of using touch exclusively as a signal for sex. This will deprive you of the warmth and physical tenderness that every marriage should have (*Love Life for Every Married Couple,* Ed Wheat. p.138).

We have yet to meet a woman who does not enjoy romance. In fact, it is safe to say that women crave it. Have you ever met a wife who begged her husband not to waste so much precious time on the unnecessary rituals of romance? You won't. That's what date nights and overnight getaways are all about, and why women love "date movies" that are hopelessly romantic. We have some friends here in Chicago who go out to a movie like clockwork every Friday night. One week he picks the movie, and the next week it is her turn. You can probably guess the variety: his night it is *Die Hard,* and for her it is *While You Were Sleeping.*

One young woman wrote this poem to her husband about her tangible need for affection:

Please—
Come take my hand
 Let's walk!!!
Give me your—
 Eyes saying—Hi!
 Glances saying—I care!
 Handholds that let me know that you were only teasing;
 Hugs saying—Thank you for being you!
 Kisses that—gently want me;
Then love—
 That says, I'll be here tomorrow
  and everyday hereafter (*Love Life,* Ed Wheat. p.136).

In an earlier chapter we highlighted Johnny Miller, president of Columbia International University as one of our hero husbands. As we wind down this chapter on keeping the romance alive in marriage, we want to close with some of his powerful words on the meaning of intimacy and its importance to the human personality:

> When I use the word, "intimacy," I am not thinking primarily of a physical relationship. Unfortunately, that is the only way much of our society understands intimacy. The fact is that two people can have a physical relationship without ever being intimate, and conversely, two people can grow into intimacy without departing into sexuality.
>
> In marriage, the ideal is to have physical oneness that grows out of spiritual and emotional oneness. That is what I mean by intimacy. It is to relate as God meant us to relate in marriage, two people becoming one. It is to be known, and still loved. Marriage provides the ideal conditions to grow in both our exposure and our commitment.
>
> Intimacy is a delightful gift. A vacuum in our personality craves it. It fills the void of loneliness. As God said, "It is not good for man to be alone." If we don't find it with our mate, we'll look for it elsewhere because life is painful without it.
>
> Such soul intimacy is the spring from which family life flows. It makes the family more than a loose collection of individuals spinning off from a common core. Intimacy is a bond of understanding that gives every family member a sense of identity: This is who I am, and I am still loved (From "Intimacy and Bucket Seats." CIU Quarterly, Winter 1996).

HERO HUSBANDS WE KNOW

When I was a little boy I remember a movie entitled *Darby O'Gill and the Little People*. Let us tell you about a friend of ours who's great at giving his wife small romantic acts of kindness. I call him "Daryl O'Bryan and the Little Romances." Experts tell us that of the various causes of depression among women, one of the most common is the combination of "loneliness, isolation, and boredom" and "an absence of romantic love." Women tend to be more romantic than men, and we men must work hard to constantly practice romance. That is what Daryl does.

What is romantic? Well, flowers are a good possibility, and negligées are romantic. Perfume is very romantic. Giving your wife a card that tells her how much you love her for no special occasion is very romantic. Or leaving her notes around the house to let her know you think about her is romantic. A phone call from work just to tell your wife you are thinking about her definitely scores high in romance.

Not long ago I was in a business meeting with Daryl O'Bryan and noticed his daytimer lying open on the place next to mine. I glanced at the notes he had in the front and saw a most amazing list. On the list were things such as "buy flowers, send a card, make a phone call, surprise her with a dinner out, candlelight, weekend getaways." It was a rather lengthy list, and when I asked him about it, I learned an excellent new technique for all of us men. "Hans," Daryl said to me, "I'm such a dummy when it comes to romance with Mary. You'd think after being married thirty years I would know how much I need to romance her to keep our marriage alive. I keep this list in front of my daytimer to constantly remind me to do the little acts of romance that will be an encouragement to her. If I don't keep looking at the list, I will just forget, and our marriage will run dry. It's my way of making it and keeping it a priority always before me."

I was so impressed with this approach that Daryl took that I have done the same thing and placed it in my own daytimer. You saw the results in chapter 2 on reminding ourselves that she is not one of the guys.

Powerpoints

Through the years of ministry and marriage, we've observed that many couples fall into the pattern of concentrating solely on work and childcare. The years when our children were babies and pre-schoolers were exhausting! I remember wondering if other couples were like us, without the energy or desire to even make love once a month! It was a relief to learn that we were not alone. But we knew it sure wasn't healthy.

So what's the ticket? How do you keep the priority of one another as #1 in your lives? First, talk it over! Set aside a date to talk through what you're both feeling and the desires you have in your relationship that are not being met.

Second, set aside a sacred "date-night" together. Try to plan one night each month for starters. Then if you get really good at it, you might progress to one night a week! Our good friends who are empty nesters find this to be no problem, of course. Since Hans and I never lived near relatives, we have always had to pay a sitter to care for our children. Since it wasn't always easy, sometimes we'd go for an economical dinner or only coffee, but we'd *go.* And Hans has learned that Donna's main desire is to debrief and build the relationship. We were thankful when the time finally came for the children to be old enough to take care of themselves.

The applications in the final chapter should seem obvious enough. Men, take the initiative to put romance back into your marriage if you have let it slip away. And remember that you will always need to make your wife feel special by doing those special little things you did before you swept her off her feet and made her your mate. Among the top things to remember:

❑ **Date your mate:** In the words of Nike, "Just Do It!"

❑ **Spend nights away at romantic getaways**: Plan your first getaway to a nice hotel or bed and breakfast. Make it a regular part of your annual schedule. It is particularly helpful at the beginning and near the end of each year to look at goals and review your progress as a couple and family.

❑ **Write her notes**: A wife never tires of getting written notes from her husband. It communicates that you took the time to actually find a card and write something. Get creative and mail it! Leave her notes when you go away on trips that she will discover while you are gone.

❑ **Spend time away from the children**: You are not shirking your responsibility, and both you and they will be better off for it. Remember that the best gift you can give your children is a great marriage.

❑ **Find common interests**: Try to do things together that are a common interest, like biking, tennis, walking, shopping for antiques, or concerts. There needs to be common interests to alleviate boredom in marriage.

❑ **Be sure to change your dating through the seasons of your marriage**: Your patterns of dating will obviously change as you go through the cycles of marriage. When the kids are little, you'll need limited objectives unless Grandma and Grandpa are around. Your goal is to have a relationship that is fun together when the children are finally gone from your nest.

❑ **Use outside resources**: David and Claudia Arp have a series of excellent seminars and resources, including the MARRIAGE ALIVE SEMINAR. Contact them through Alive Communications, Colorado Springs, CO (719) 260-7080. Also see their excellent marriage dating books; *The Ultimate Marriage Builder,* and *52 Dates for You and Your Mate* (Thomas Nelson, 1994 and 1993).

Remember:
All work and no play can make
marriages a very dull place to be.

REFERENCES CITED

Allen, Tim.
  Don't Stand Too Close to a Naked Man, New York: Hyperion Publishers, 1994.

Dillow, Linda.
  Creative Counterpart, Nashville: Thomas Nelson, 1977.

Harley, Willard F., Jr.
  His Needs, Her Needs, Grand Rapids: Fleming H. Revell, 1994.
  Used with permission.

Kennerly, Paul.
  "Give a Little Love," (Words and music) 1988 Rondor Music (London) Ltd.
  (PRS) Administered by Irving Music, Inc. (BMI) in U.S.A. and Canada. All
  rights reserved, used by permission. WARNER BROS. PUBLICATIONS
  U.S. INC., Miami, FL 33014.

Logan, Jim.
  Reclaiming Surrendered Ground, Chicago: Moody Press, 1995.

McQuilken, Robertson.
  "Muriel's Blessing," *Christianity Today*, February 1996.

Ryan, Ruth.
  Covering Home, Waco: Word Books, as quoted on page 87, *Reader's Digest*,
  September, 1995.

Smalley, Gary.
  If Only He Knew, Grand Rapids: Zondervan, 1982.

Smith, Jim.
  Learning to Live with the One You Love, Carol Stream, IL: Tyndale House, 1991.
  Used with permission.

Swindoll, Charles.
  Woman: A Person of Worth and Dignity, Portland, OR: Multnomah Press, 1983.

Walvoord, John F., and Roy Zuck.
The Bible Knowledge Commentary, Wheaton, IL: Victor Books, 1989.

Wheat, Ed.
Love Life for Every Married Couple, Grand Rapids: Zondervan, 1980. Used with permission.

Wiersbe, Warren.
"Be Rich," *The Bible Exposition Commentary*, Wheaton: Victor Books, 1989.